A Practical Guide to Mental Health Law
in Hong Kong

A Practical Guide to Mental Health Law in Hong Kong

Sherlynn G. Chan

Hong Kong University Press
The University of Hong Kong
Pokfulam Road
Hong Kong
https://hkupress.hku.hk

© 2019 Hong Kong University Press

ISBN 978-988-8528-15-8 (*Hardback*)
ISBN 978-988-8528-16-5 (*Paperback*)

All rights reserved. No portion of this publication may be reproduced or transmitted in any form or by any means, electronic or mechanical, including photocopying, recording, or any information storage or retrieval system, without prior permission in writing from the publisher.

British Library Cataloguing-in-Publication Data
A catalogue record for this book is available from the British Library.

10 9 8 7 6 5 4 3 2

Printed and bound by Paramount Printing Co. Ltd., Hong Kong, China

In memory of my father, Rev. Dr. Jachin Yin Man Chan

Contents

Foreword	ix
Preface	x
Acknowledgements	xiii

Part I

Chapter 1: Case Studies	3
Chapter 2: A Brief Overview of the Mental Health Ordinance (Cap 136)	18
Documents	
Practice Direction 30.1	27
Practice Direction 18.1 (Extract)	32
Chapter 3: Committee versus Guardian	37
Chapter 4: Mental Capacity	50

Part II

Chapter 5: Ways to Protect and Manage the Mentally Incapacitated Person's (**MIP**) Property and Affairs	63
Chapter 6: Practical Considerations on How to Manage Assets of the MIP	73
Documents	
Guidance Note to Persons Appointed as Committee of Estate of a Mentally Incapacitated Person	81
Sample Draft Order for Relief Sought	87

Part III

Chapter 7: Other Planning Tools: Enduring Power of Attorney, Advance Directive, and Continuing Power of Attorney	95
Documents	
Enduring Power of Attorney—Form 1	102
Enduring Power of Attorney—Form 2	110
Sample Advance Directive Form	120

Chapter 8: Will or No Will?	124
Chapter 9: Hong Kong and Beyond	132
Chapter 10: The Way Forward	138
Appendix I: Useful Glossary of Legal and Medical Terms	143
Appendix II: Useful List of Government and Non-government Resources Available in Hong Kong	147

Foreword

People who lost their mental capacities are vulnerable and the law should protect them from being exploited. At the same time, it can be quite taxing for those who take care of such persons and the law should not unduly burden such carers with administrative duties on them. Further, different members in the family of such a person can have different views on what are the best for that person. Sometimes, for one reason or another, such differences cannot be resolved amongst these members by themselves. In those cases, the law needs to provide an efficient and effective means to resolve such differences. Though Hong Kong does not have a Court of Protection, our mental health law has undergone quite significant developments in the past decade. With the promulgation of Practice Direction 30.1 in 2005, there have been more cases coming to court for the establishment of committees for mentally incapacitated persons and the court has examined many aspects of the supervisory jurisdiction under Part II of the Mental Health Ordinance and its interactions with other authorities monitoring the welfare of those persons like the Guardianship Board and the Director of Social Welfare. It is therefore opportune for a book on mental health law in Hong Kong to be published. Sherlynn Chan must be congratulated for her efforts in this work which represents a substantial contribution to the promotion of the sound and proper engagement of the legal process in this area. It is a work which provides useful and up-to-date guidance to practitioners in this field. I would highly recommend it to lawyers and students.

The Honourable Mr Justice Johnson Lam Man Hon
Vice-President of the Court of Appeal of the High Court

Preface

Did you know that, as a result of Hong Kong's ageing population, about one-third of us will be aged 65 or above by 2036?[1] Meanwhile, life expectancy will increase to 87 for men and over 90 for women in Hong Kong![2]

Yet medical experts predict that around one in ten people aged 65 years old or above and around one in three aged 80 or above will likely suffer from dementia, a common cause of mental incapacity.[3]

In other words, many of us will be looking after a family member incapacitated by some form of mental disease, most commonly dementia, for nearly 30 years. From my personal experience, I know how tough it is to take care of a family member who is mentally incapacitated.

When I was 16 years old, I learned that my 70-year-old paternal grandmother was suffering from dementia. I saw how difficult it was for my father to find home care assistance until she passed away at the age of 80.

On many occasions, my grandmother accused our domestic helpers of stealing her personal items when she had simply misplaced them. The helpers left one after another as my grandmother's condition worsened.

Looking back, I can appreciate the enormous stress my father was under whilst trying to strike a balance between his career, his volunteer work and looking after our family with limited assistance.

In those days, there were not many medical specialists and elderly centres providing specialized care for dementia patients. I saw how my father, who was amazingly patient, tried to persuade my grandmother time and again to seek medical help, particularly after she had a mini-stroke and

---

1. See the Hong Kong Population Projections 2015–2064 prepared by the Census and Statistics Department of the Hong Kong government for further information.
2. Ibid.
3. See Hospital Authority's Smart Patient website, available at www21.ha.org.hk; Laura Chung's article "Everything about Dementia in Hong Kong", available at jmsc.hku.hk; and the research article "Trends in Prevalence and Mortality of Dementia in Elderly Hong Kong Population: Projections, Disease Burden, and Implications for Long-Term Care" jointly written by Ruby Yu, Pui Hing Chau, Sarah M. McGhee, Wai Ling Cheung, Kam Che Chan, Sai Hei Cheung, and Jean Woo.

when she started to suffer from double incontinence. The tension within my family when my grandmother repeatedly refused help at that time still lingers in my mind now.

Fortunately, compared with the old days, the Hong Kong government and non-governmental organizations have spared no effort to provide support to the mentally incapacitated, their families and carers. Nevertheless, there is still a need for Hong Kong to develop a more advanced legal framework and social welfare system to protect the physical and financial well-being of people with special needs. I also believe that we can all contribute to supporting special needs persons at the individual level.

Throughout my 25-year legal career in private practice and in the Legal Aid Department, including working in the Official Solicitor's Office, I have focused on family-related proceedings, estate planning, wealth protection and representing mentally incapacitated persons, in both contentious and non-contentious situations. After leaving the government, my interest in and concern for private clients and family work have continued, as an accredited family and general mediator in private practice, while also serving for a period as Deputy District Judge in the Family Court of Hong Kong.

Thanks to my work, I have gained a deep understanding of the problems encountered by special needs persons and helped resolve the thorny issues faced by their carers and families. In one case, a lady was faced with a tenant who refused to deposit the rent into a joint bank account held with her mother. Her mother was hospitalized and could no longer speak coherently. The tenant therefore tried to take advantage of her mother's mental incapacity and refused to pay rent. At that time, not many lawyers were aware of what the lady could do legally to require the tenant to fulfil his contractual obligation. The lady felt helpless and suffered emotional distress as she was faced with her mother's huge medical bills.

In another case, a caretaker of a private residential building talked an elderly lady who had no surviving family members or relatives into transferring her apartment to him when she was in hospital. Luckily, the medical social worker who was suspicious of the matter immediately reported to and sought help from the Official Solicitor and the court to protect the elderly lady from financial abuse. From these cases, I realized that we, as legal professionals, must work harder to safeguard the interests of the mentally incapacitated.

Furthermore, as a volunteer worker for many years, I have had the chance to interact with special needs children and have been made aware of the numerous challenges facing their families. As far as I know, Hong Kong families with special needs children, such as those with severe autism or Down syndrome, are often anxious about who will look after their children when they themselves grow old, become physically challenged or potentially develop some form of impairment of the brain.

In light of the ageing population and increased life expectancy, I believe that we will see a surge in the number of cases involving people looking after their mentally incapacitated family members. We must all prepare for the upcoming challenges before it is too late.

In writing this guide, I aim to raise the general awareness of this area of law, which is very important but seldom discussed, even amongst legal practitioners, so that carers and professionals who work with special needs persons will have support and practical guidance as to how and when to seek legal assistance.

This guide is divided into three parts:

Part I consists of 12 modified case studies based on real-life scenarios, providing an introduction to the relevant mental health law in Hong Kong.

Part II highlights the legal procedures and practical considerations as to how to manage the property and affairs of persons with special needs and/ or mental incapacitation.

Part III outlines some other planning tools such as wills, enduring powers of attorney, the emerging continuing power of attorney and advance medical directives, and explores the way forward for Hong Kong with reference to other common law jurisdictions.

A glossary of common legal and medical terms as well as a list of government and non-government resources available in Hong Kong are annexed at the end of the book for easy reference.

I hope you will enjoy reading this guide and find it both interesting and helpful.

Acknowledgements

I would like to thank all the people who have made this book a reality.

I would like to express my heartfelt gratitude to the co-founders of MIP Care Resources Connect (a newly incorporated charitable organization in Hong Kong)—Celeste, Elim, Jess, Teresa, Thelma, Gladys, and Frances—for sharing the same vision of helping carers of people with special needs navigate through the available resources in Hong Kong and for raising awareness on this increasingly important topic within the community.

I am especially grateful to Celeste, whose love and dedication for her family, faith, and positivism in everything she does have inspired me to write this book.

I thank HKU Press's editing and marketing team—Clara, Susie, Winnie, and Jen—who have helpfully guided me through the publication process and patiently answered the questions of a novice author; the anonymous peer reviewers who have given me the most valuable comments; and my friends and copyeditors—Oswald, Trish, Sarina and Larina—who have helped me at different stages to make sure each chapter is as accurate and appropriate as it can be.

I thank my former HKU LLB classmates, especially Alice, Edmund, Lusina, and Tony, for their encouragement that I should take on and finish this book project despite the challenges.

I thank my colleagues, Catherine and Hazel, without whom I would not have been able to write this book while working full-time in private client legal work. I am especially indebted to Hazel who has stood by my side and cheered me on to the finish line.

I am very grateful for my fellow delinquent moms, Frances and Tina, who have helped me keep my sanity as a working mom, sharing the much needed cup of coffee after dropping the kids off to school to keep me going throughout the day.

My husband, Andy has been the pillar of support to this book. I cannot thank him enough for his unconditional love and support throughout this journey and for tolerating many of my midnight disappearances into the study room; and to my three children, Jethro, Nathaniel, and Ashley who always wonder why mum turns up late for dinner.

Last but not least, I give thanks to my Heavenly Father, who is the author of all knowledge and the source of my strength and vision.

Part I

1
Case Studies

Over the years, I have seen many cases involving families with members who are suffering from some form of behavioural challenge, such as autism, dementia and other brain diseases, and subjected to financial abuse by others, some by their own family members and/or their care-givers.

Here are some modified case studies based on real life scenarios for you to consider. You may be able to identify some common issues faced by these people and their family members, and wonder what families can do to protect their loved ones from financial abuse and what plans they can make in the best interests of their loved ones who are unable to make decisions for themselves in various situations.

This practical guide is intended to provide some basic knowledge on how to protect your loved ones who lack the mental capacity to make reasoned decisions for themselves, whether on their personal welfare or financial affairs.

If you encounter similar situations or are interested to find out more about these issues, please seek appropriate legal advice and/or contact relevant organizations or government departments with your enquiries.

Case Study 1: The Young Man Who Inherited a Property

> *Mr and Mrs A are in their late 50s. They have one child, X, who was diagnosed with severe autism and global development delay since childhood. X is now 25 years old and continues to suffer from autistic spectrum disorder and epilepsy and has a mental age of 10 years old. X just inherited a residential property in Hong Kong from his paternal grandfather who passed away recently.*
>
> *The solicitors handling the probate matters for X's paternal grandfather are concerned that X does not have the mental capacity to understand and sign legal documents for the transfer of the property into his name.*

> Mr and Mrs A are also concerned that their son may be a target for financial abuse when they themselves grow old and can no longer look after X.

Subsequent Developments

This scenario is not uncommon. Many couples with special needs children are concerned with who will look after their children when they themselves grow old and are no longer able to look after their special needs children. The solicitors handling the probate matters and intended transfer were correct to raise concerns about the mental capacity of X to sign the legal documents.

Based on the above concerns, Mr and Mrs A made enquiries as to what options they had and eventually decided to instruct solicitors to take out a Part II application under the Mental Health Ordinance (Cap 136) (**MHO**) to apply to the Mental Health Court in Hong Kong for an order that Mrs A be appointed as the committee of the estate (**Committee**) of X to manage the property and financial affairs of X.

The Mental Health Court conferred various powers on the Committee as set out in a court order, including, among other things, the power to sign the necessary legal documents for the transfer of the property inherited from X's paternal grandfather to X; renting out the property; and depositing the rental income into the Committee's account for X's use and benefit, which included payment of X's medical and other therapy fees.

Mrs A understood that she had to file annual accounts to the court and was more than happy to do so, since she felt that she was creating a blueprint to facilitate others to take over in future when she is no longer capable of looking after her son.

For more information on the scope and powers of a committee, refer to Chapter 3 and Practice Direction 30.1 (**PD 30.1**).[1]

Case Study 2: The Elderly Businessman

> *Mr Y's three sons all work in the same family business which was founded by Mr Y in the 1950s. Mr Y is in his mid-80s but still relatively healthy and walks to work every day. His wife passed away almost 10 years ago.*
>
> *One morning, when Mr Y was walking to work, he was hit by a car whilst crossing the street and fell into a coma. He was then hospitalized for many months.*
>
> *While Mr Y's sons were helping their father sort out his bank statements and credit card payments, they discovered that their father had opened several new personal accounts in recent months and Mr Y's secretary alerted them of some irregular lump sum withdrawals from one of Mr Y's new personal bank accounts since the car accident.*
>
> *The sons subsequently discovered that one of Mr Y's female business partners, Ms C, had been in a close relationship with Mr Y and residing in one of his investment properties rent free for about eight years prior to the accident.*

Subsequent Developments

Although Mr Y's medical condition improved and he came out of the coma, he was unable to speak coherently. Due to severe brain damage, he required 24 hour nursing care, regular physiotherapy, occupational therapy and speech therapy.

Mr Y's sons initially wanted to make a report to the police regarding the "unauthorized" lump sum withdrawals, but after speaking to their father's accountant and making enquiries with the bank and third parties, they discovered that Ms C had Mr Y's written authorization to operate the new personal accounts opened by Mr Y in recent years, and decided otherwise.

Mr Y's three sons agreed that they would apply jointly to be the Committee of Mr Y under Part II of the MHO to protect their father from

---

1. Practice Direction 30.1 dated 10 October 2005, issued by the Hong Kong Judiciary.

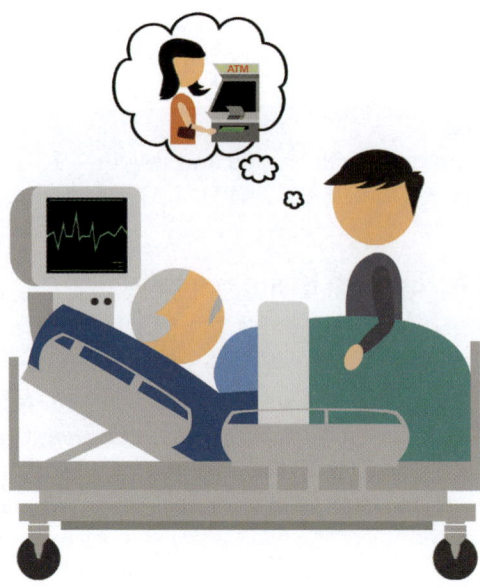

financial abuse and to properly manage the family business, properties and other financial affairs of their father.

Case Study 3: The Wealthy Widow

> Mrs Z is a 78-year-old widow without any children. She inherited substantial assets when her husband passed away. She has some nieces and nephews residing in Hong Kong and some in the mainland. They all visit her regularly. Mrs Z was recently diagnosed with dementia and hospitalized after she had a stroke.
>
> There have been disputes between Mrs Z's nieces and nephews (who are divided into two groups, "**Camp A**" and "**Camp B**") regarding whether Mrs Z should return to her own home after being discharged from hospital and stay with one of her nieces who had been looking after her before she had a stroke, or whether she should be transferred to an elderly home with around-the-clock nursing care and a resident doctor.
>
> One of the nieces from Camp A applied to the Guardianship Board to be appointed as Mrs Z's guardian, but this was disputed by the legal representatives of Camp B. At the same time, the nephew from Camp B applied for a Committee Order to be appointed as the Committee to manage the property and affairs of Mrs Z.

Case Studies

Subsequent Developments

The two camps of nieces and nephews both considered their representative to be the more appropriate person to be appointed as the guardian of Mrs Z under Part IVB of the MHO. Since the documents were not in order, the Guardianship Board was unable to set the date for the hearing and the parties became anxious when the doctor at the hospital advised that Mrs Z was ready to be discharged.

Meanwhile, a Part II application under the MHO for a Committee to be appointed for Mrs Z was taken out by a nephew from Camp B, but the application was opposed by the nieces and nephews in Camp A. Fortunately, despite their antagonistic approach in court, the parties soon realized that the best possible solution for both camps in the circumstances was to appoint an independent Committee.

When an independent Committee was appointed and met with both camps, all the nieces and nephews agreed that it was in the best interests of Mrs Z to be discharged from hospital immediately and transferred to an elderly home with appropriate nursing care.

Shortly thereafter, at the Guardianship Board hearing, the Board assessed the medical reports, social enquiry report and opposing views regarding the care and accommodation arrangements, and ordered that a public guardian, ie the Director of Social Welfare, was the most appropriate person to be appointed as guardian of Mrs Z.

Case Study 4: The Medical Professional Who Suffered a Stroke

> Dr H was a highly successful doctor in a private clinic before he suffered a double stroke at the age of 55. He did not prepare any will or enduring power of attorney. He is not married, but has had several female companions. Dr H's parents passed away several years ago and he does not have any siblings.
>
> Dr P, the close business partner and friend of Dr H, decided to make an application to the Guardianship Board to be Dr H's guardian, and made arrangements for Dr H to be transferred to a hospice care centre immediately after he was discharged from hospital.
>
> However, one of Dr H's female companions, Ms W, was dissatisfied with Dr P's care arrangements and wanted to replace Dr P as Dr H's guardian.

Subsequent Developments

After Dr P was appointed as guardian of Dr H, he made detailed care arrangements for Dr H at the hospice care centre, including employing a private registered nurse, a physiotherapist, an occupational therapist and a speech therapist to look after Dr H.

Whilst Dr P used his best endeavours to make appropriate care arrangements for Dr H and visited Dr H once every two weeks, he was criticized by Ms W, one of Dr H's female companions who visited Dr H regularly, that the needs of Dr H were being neglected.

Ms W also disagreed with the frequency of private physiotherapy and other treatments arranged by Dr P and wanted to remove Dr P as Dr H's guardian. She therefore made a request to the Guardianship Board to review the Guardianship Order.

Guardianship Orders are reviewed and renewed regularly by the Guardianship Board and the Board will look at what is in the best interests of the patient/concerned person and not the personal preference of one family member over the other.[2] In this case, the Guardianship Board obtained a social enquiry report, reviewed updated medical reports and renewed the Guardianship Order in favour of Dr P.

---

2. See s 59U and s 59O of Part IVB of the MHO and the website of the Guardianship Board, available at http://www.adultguardianship.org.hk/admin/Data/uploadfile/174/L2Erev4.pdf.

Case Study 5: The Undiscovered Talent of an Autistic Street Sleeper

> *Mr D was a street sleeper. A bystander saw him wandering on the street, talking to himself and banging his head against the wall until his head was bleeding. The bystander called the ambulance to take Mr D to hospital and reported the incident to the police. Mr D was subsequently diagnosed by a government psychiatrist with severe cognitive disorder and intellectual disability.*
>
> *The Director of Social Welfare was asked to prepare a social enquiry report at the Guardianship Board hearing, during which they found out that Mr D's father had passed away recently and had set up a trust naming Mr D as the sole beneficiary under the trust. The Director of Social Welfare also discovered that Mr D is an autistic savant with exceptional talent in playing the piano and painting.*

Subsequent Developments

The trustees under the trust set up by the late father of Mr D were immediately notified of Mr D's condition. The trustees then applied to the court for an order appointing them as Committee of Mr D and a public guardian was also appointed to look after his welfare and arrangements.

In view of Mr D's condition and preference, the public guardian made arrangements for him to reside in a government-subsidized hostel in Yuen Long, which allowed Mr D to work in a sheltered environment and go on outings and even overseas trips with other members, together with well-trained staff and social workers.

The social worker looking after the welfare of Mr D noted Mr D's talents. He was able to arrange art exhibitions for Mr D at the hostel and often displayed Mr D's artwork on the walls of the hostel. He also invited Mr D to play the piano during festive celebrations and parties.

Case Study 6: The Celebrity with Brain Cancer

> *Mr K is a celebrity who was diagnosed with brain cancer last year at the age of 39. His health deteriorated rapidly and during a recent media interview on his battle with cancer, his speech was not coherent and he was slurring. Mr K's parents, sister and close friends were concerned about his ability to make reasonable decisions in relation to his personal circumstances, in particular giving consent to medical treatment and handling his finances.*

> *When he was admitted to hospital, he refused to receive any form of treatment for his cancer and insisted that no one should have any right to make any decision for him. He said that he was prepared to die anytime and did not want to be subjected to any pain or surgery.*
>
> *The doctors at the hospital certified that Mr K was mentally incapacitated and unable to make reasonable decisions for his well-being. Mr K's family members immediately applied for an Emergency Guardianship Order so they could make immediate provisions to protect Mr K.*

Subsequent Developments

The family members and close friends of Mr K all held different views. Some believed that Mr K should be allowed to refuse any form of invasive or non-invasive medical treatment and be allowed to make his own decision as to how to live or end his life with dignity, while some believed that Mr K was incapable of understanding the general nature and effect of the proposed treatment and the decision to refuse medical treatment was unreasonable and might be detrimental to his well-being.

Since Mr K was certified by two medical practitioners that he was mentally incapacitated and incapable of making reasonable decisions in respect of matters which related to his personal circumstances, it was possible for his family members to apply for an Emergency Guardianship Order and make immediate provisions to protect Mr K, which was what happened.

Case Study 7: The Elderly Landlady

> *Mr and Mrs G have one adult son. After Mr G passed away, he left Mrs G with two properties in Hong Kong and a significant sum of cash.*
>
> *Not long after Mr G had passed away, Mrs G suffered a stroke and her son started to look after her and take care of all her medical arrangements and expenses. One of the tenants refused to pay rent after learning that Mr G had passed away and Mrs G was hospitalized.*
>
> *The son threatened to take legal action against the tenant if the latter continued to refuse to pay rent. He made an application to be appointed as the Committee of Mrs G and sought, among other things, the right to issue legal proceedings against the tenant on behalf of Mrs G as her next friend.*
>
> *However, during the application process Mrs G's son discovered that Mrs G had prepared a will giving all her estate to her favourite charity and appointed her private banker to be the executor, leaving nothing for him.*

Subsequent Developments

The son was shocked that his mother prepared a will leaving nothing to him and raised queries with the private banker to ascertain the reason why Mrs G would make such a will. Whilst the private banker showed understanding, he was not willing to assist or answer the son's queries.

An independent Committee was appointed under Part II of the MHO for Mrs G, and enquiries were made as to the circumstances of the making of Mrs G's will.

In the end, the court, having considered the circumstances of the case and with paramount consideration given to Mrs G's welfare and requirements, approved the execution of a statutory will to avoid the high possibility of an expensive probate action after her demise between the son, the private banker and the charity as beneficiary.

If you are interested in this topic, refer to the judgment in *Re CYL* (HCMP No 2567/2005), where the court authorized the execution of a statutory will and set out the reasons for exercising its discretion to direct the execution after considering the complexity of the matter, the stance of the parties and assessment of the mentally incapacitated person's requirements and sections 10B(1)(e) and 10C of the MHO.

Case Study 8: The Retired Widower with Family Residing Overseas

> *Mr F is a retired wealthy businessman. His wife passed away recently. He has six adult children, five of whom live with their own families in Canada, Singapore and Australia. Only the youngest son, Mr N, and daughter in law live in Hong Kong with Mr F.*
>
> *When Mr F started to show signs of dementia, his youngest son and family in Hong Kong started to alienate Mr F from friends and relatives. The other siblings heard from friends living in Hong Kong that they had not seen Mr F for many months and were concerned about his well-being. When they called their brother and sister in law in Hong Kong, they refused to answer the phone and responded in e-mail that their parents were doing fine and refused to take Mr F to see the doctor.*
>
> *When the eldest sister and her family members came to Hong Kong, they were not allowed to visit their father and grandfather. She later found out from her father's domestic helper, who was employed by Mr N to care for Mr F, that Mr F had not left the home for two years and no one was allowed to enter the house without her employer's permission.*

Subsequent Developments

The other family members and close friends of Mr F were made aware of the situation. Since Mr N was very hostile and uncooperative to all his siblings and other family members, the other family members sought advice from solicitors in Hong Kong.

Eventually, Mr N agreed to take Mr F to be assessed by a doctor and produced a medical report to confirm that while Mr F showed early signs of dementia, he was still capable of managing his property and affairs. Mr F's other family members subsequently obtained contrary medical evidence as to the mental capacity of Mr F, and thus took out an application under Part II of the MHO for a Committee to be appointed for Mr F.

The court set down a two-day hearing to determine whether Mr F was mentally incapacitated for the purpose of appointing a Committee under Part II of the MHO. The court, having considered the medical reports and heard evidence from the medical experts, the siblings and Mr F himself, decided that Mr F was incapable of handling his property and affairs.

If you are interested in reading more on this topic, refer to Chapter 4 on mental capacity.

Case Study 9: The Young Businesswoman

Ms M was a highly successful business woman who owned several landed properties in Hong Kong. When she was on holiday in Europe, she suffered from severe allergy which resulted in suffocation and subsequent brain damage. She had not prepared any will or enduring power of attorney.

Ms M's brother made arrangements for Ms M to return to Hong Kong and she has been in a coma since returning to Hong Kong. Ms M's brother applied to the court for an order to sell one of Ms M's properties to pay for the private hospital's fees which exceeded HK$100,000 per month.

However, Ms M's brother discovered that Ms M had, unbeknownst to her family, been maintaining her boyfriend.

Subsequent Developments

Since Ms M did not execute any enduring power of attorney in Hong Kong, a Part II application under the MHO was initiated by her brother.

Ms M's boyfriend subsequently made an application to the court for maintenance from Ms M's estate. Since he was able to prove that, had Ms M not been mentally incapacitated, she would have continued to provide for

Case Studies

his rent and utilities, the court made an order for monthly payment to Ms M's boyfriend in such amount as it deemed appropriate.[3]

The Committee therefore followed the court order to manage the financial affairs of Ms M including the monthly payment to her boyfriend.

Case Study 10: The Husband in Matrimonial Proceedings

Mrs E issued divorce proceedings against Mr E on the grounds of unreasonable behaviour and domestic violence. Mrs E revealed to her solicitors that around three years ago, Mr E had begun suffering from personality adjustment disorder and depression after he was laid off by his employer during the financial crisis, after which he saw a psychiatrist and received treatment for a period of about 15 months.

The solicitors for Mrs E were concerned about Mr E's mental fitness to defend the ancillary relief claims under the divorce proceedings after serving the petition for divorce on him and suggested that Mr E be assessed by a psychiatrist to see if he was fit to give instructions in the proceedings.

However, Mr E refused to see any doctor and insisted that he did not need any legal representation in the divorce proceedings.

---

3. See s 10A (c) of the MHO.

Subsequent Developments

Mrs E's solicitors obtained a direction from the court that the Official Solicitor be asked to make enquiries with the relevant government psychiatrist as to whether or not Mr E was fit to give instructions. Since the medical evidence obtained confirmed that Mr E was not fit to give instructions and defend his rather complex ancillary relief claim, the court appointed the Official Solicitor to be Mr E's guardian ad litem (guardian for the purposes of the legal proceedings) because there was no suitable next of kin who was willing to act in that role.[4]

It is important to note that the court may, in appropriate cases, direct the Official Solicitor to consider giving his consent to be a party's guardian ad litem and/or make enquiry as to that party's mental capacity or fitness to give instructions in divorce and other legal proceedings.

Case Study 11: The Child Who Suffered Serious Injuries in a Car Accident

> *Mr and Mrs B have three daughters and one son, aged 6, 8, 13, and 16 respectively. Their 8-year-old daughter, AB, was knocked down by a truck when she was walking back home from school with her elder sister and suffered severe brain damage. AB underwent numerous operations. Her cognitive and speech functions have been severely damaged.*
>
> *The doctors told Mr and Mrs B that their daughter has dystonic quadriplegic cerebral palsy and will be dependent on gastrostomy feeding and specialist care for the rest of her life.*
>
> *The truck driver was charged with and convicted of the offence of reckless driving causing serious bodily harm. Mr and Mrs B applied for legal aid and took out a personal injuries claim against the driver and a rather large settlement was reached and approved by the High Court.*

Subsequent Developments

Mrs B acted on AB's behalf to commence a personal injuries claim against the driver and the motor insurers. Her lawyers also made an application under Part II of the MHO for Mrs B to be appointed as Committee of AB. She was legally represented at all times and a substantial settlement sum was approved by the court with her lawyers' advice, and the money was duly paid by the motor insurers.

---

4. See r 105(5) of the Matrimonial Causes Rules (Cap 179A).

Unfortunately, neither Mrs B nor any of the family members of AB had practical knowledge on how to properly map out the care regime for AB or how to seek appropriate help after AB's personal injuries claim was settled.

Mrs B as Committee of AB applied to the Mental Health Court for directions to engage a case manager to map out a comprehensive care regime for AB, as well as a financial consultant for the Committee to advise on how to invest the settlement sum or any part thereof, to ensure that AB would be able to get better care and necessary treatment and protection.

Refer to Chapter 5 on "persons with acquired brain injury due to accidents" to read more on this topic.

Case Study 12: The Paraplegic Construction Worker

> Mr Q was a construction worker who suffered severe injuries in an industrial accident rendering him a paraplegic. He was the breadwinner of the family with three young children. His wife received formal education up to primary school and looks after the children on a full time basis.
>
> A social worker accompanied Mr Q's wife to apply for legal aid to take out proceedings against the employer for compensation. Mr Q's wife also applied to be appointed as Committee of Mr Q.

> *However, when a substantial settlement sum was awarded to Mr Q at the conclusion of the court proceedings, it was transpired that Mrs Q had started to suffer from severe depression and other personality disorders.*

Subsequent Developments

Since Mrs Q was suffering from depression and personality disorders, it soon became clear to the other family members, the doctors and her legal representatives that she was not fit to continue to act as Committee of Mr Q. Thus, the court appointed Mr Q's sister, who had no interest adverse to Mr Q, to replace Mrs Q as the Committee.

Further Analysis

While legal aid in Hong Kong is available to help victims of traffic and industrial accidents to issue proceedings against the wrongdoer, it is usually limited to reaching a settlement or award and does not cover the costs relating to setting up a Committee with a proper care regime.

Thus it can be difficult for family members of victims who have suffered very serious injuries to acquire knowledge of how to set up the Committee and apply for money to be released from the court to set up a proper care regime for the victims after conclusion of legal proceedings. Unlike professional Committees, many laypersons find it difficult to find such assistance.

When large sums of money are paid into the court intended to provide better care and treatment for the victims, they should not lie idle in the Suitors' Fund in court, which happens often.

To read more on this topic, see the reasons for decision in *Fong Yau Hei v Gammon Construction Limited et al*, in particular the comments and reminder to practitioners in the field of personal injury litigation made by Mr Justice Bharwaney.[5]

---

5. Decision dated 25 October 2017 (HCPI No 1222/2003), paras 14 to 19 and 53 to 56.

2
A Brief Overview of the Mental Health Ordinance (Cap 136)

The Mental Health Ordinance (Cap 136) (**MHO**) was first enacted in 1962. It is essentially the consolidation of all statutory provisions relating to the protection of mentally incapacitated persons in respect of their health care, consent to medical treatment and management of their property and affairs. "Property and affairs" generally refers to business matters, legal transactions and other dealings of a similar kind.

While a number of amendments have been made to the MHO since its enactment, Hong Kong is still very slow in developing this area of law and many of the concepts used are rather archaic compared to the mental health legislation in other common law jurisdictions.

I will highlight some of the main concerns and inadequacies in this area of law in the final chapter. In this chapter I will provide a brief overview of the existing statutory provisions and Part II and Part IVB of the MHO.

In short, the aim and purpose of the MHO are:[1]

> 1) to amend and consolidate the law relating to mental incapacity and the care and supervision of mentally incapacitated persons;
> 2) to provide for the management of the property and affairs of mentally incapacitated persons;
> 3) to provide for the reception, detention and treatment of mentally incapacitated persons who are mentally disordered persons or patients;
> 4) to provide for the guardianship of such patients and for mentally incapacitated persons in general;
> 5) to make provision for the giving of consent for treatment or special treatment in respect of mentally incapacitated persons who have attained 18 years of age;

---

1. As stated in the long title of the MHO.

6) to provide for the removal of objectionable terminology relating to mental incapacity in other statutory provisions; and
7) to provide for matters incidental or consequential thereto.

The MHO is divided into 10 parts, each dealing with different aspects of the law relating to mentally incapacitated persons:

- Part I—Preliminary (sections 1 to 6)
- Part II—Management of Property and Affairs of Mentally Incapacitated Persons (sections 7 to 28)
- Part III—Reception, Detention and Treatment of Patients (sections 29 to 44)
- Part IIIA—Guardianship of Persons Concerned in Criminal Proceedings (sections 44A to 44B)
- Part IIIB—Supervision and Treatment Orders Relating to Persons Concerned in Criminal Proceedings (sections 44C to 44I)
- Part IV—Admission of Mentally Disordered Persons Concerned in Criminal Proceedings, Transfer of Mentally Disordered Persons under Sentence and Remand of Mentally Incapacitated Persons (sections 45 to 59)
- Part IVA—Mental Health Review Tribunal (sections 59A to 59H)
- Part IVB—Guardianship (sections 59I to 59Z)
- Part IVC—Medical and Dental Treatment (sections 59ZA to 59ZK)
- Part V—General Provisions (sections 60 to 74)

Protection versus Deprivation of Liberty under the MHO

There are lively discussions amongst academics and experts internationally on the human rights issues arising from the involuntary treatment and detention of mentally incapacitated persons. There is concern as to whether some of the provisions in the MHO, such as those dealing with involuntary treatment and compulsory detention, may violate the Universal Declaration of Human Rights (**UDHR**).

For example, Article 12 of the UDHR provides that "no one shall be subject to arbitrary interference with his privacy, family, home or correspondence, nor to attacks upon his honour and reputation. Everyone has the right to the protection of the law against such interference or attacks".[2]

---

2. See Article 12 of the UDHR, available at www.ohchr.org.

Article 12(4) of the Convention on Rights of Persons with Disabilities (**CRPD**) provides that:

> All measures that relate to the exercise of legal capacity provide for appropriate and effective safeguards to prevent abuse in accordance with international human rights law. Such safeguards shall ensure that measures relating to the exercise of legal capacity respect the rights, will and preferences of the person, are free of conflict of interest and undue influence, are proportional and tailored to the person's circumstances, apply for the shortest time possible and are subject to regular review by a competent, independent and impartial authority or judicial body. The safeguards shall be proportional to the degree to which such measures affect the person's rights and interests.

Article 14 of the CRPD also provides that:

> State Parties shall ensure that persons with disabilities, on an equal basis with others: a) enjoy the right to liberty and security of person; and b) are not deprived of their liberty unlawfully or arbitrarily and that any deprivation of liberty is in conformity with the law, and that the existence of a disability shall in no case justify a deprivation of liberty.

In 2012, Hong Kong had approximately 800 patients detained at the psychiatric in-patient units due to medical evidence that the patient was suffering from a mental disorder of a nature or degree which warranted his or her detention in a mental hospital for observation.[3] It has been argued that the legal threshold for detaining a patient "for observation" under sections 31 and 32 of the MHO is very low.

Section 31(1) of the MHO provides that:

> An application may be made to a District Judge or Magistrate for an order for the detention of a patient for observation on the grounds that the patient a) is suffering from mental disorder of a nature or degree which warrants his detention in a mental hospital for observation (or for observation followed by medical treatment) for at least a limited period; and b) ought to be so detained in the interests of his own health or safety or with a view to the protection of other persons.

The application under this section is based on the written opinion of a registered medical practitioner who has examined the individual concerned within the previous seven days and, unless the individual requests, the judge or magistrate does not need to see the individual.

---

3. The Human Rights Committee requested and responded to the review on the provisions and operation of the MHO. See "Unfinished Business: Reforming Hong Kong's Mental Health Ordinance to Comply with International Norms", available at http://www.cmel.hku.hk/wp-content/uploads/2017/04/Day-1-Presentation-3-Professor-Carole-Petersen.pdf.

Hence, there needs to be a fine balance between "protection" of an individual and "deprivation" of the individual's liberty when considering whether the compulsory mental health treatment of a patient is necessary. We must therefore ask ourselves whether the involuntary treatment and compulsory detention are necessary for the patient's own good (a "prevention of harm to self" justification) or whether it is necessary for the protection of others from the patient but not necessarily for the patient's own good (a "prevention of harm to others" justification).

It is therefore understandable that some human rights lawyers will argue that Part II of the MHO may be in violation of several provisions of the UDHR and/or the CRPD.

While this is a very important topic, particularly given that the current legislation is based on rather archaic concepts and outdated compared with other jurisdictions, this book is mainly written from the carer's perspective and will focus on the care and management of special needs and mentally incapacitated persons under Part II and Part IVB of the MHO.

Part II and Part IVB of the MHO

As mentioned, Part II of the MHO deals with the "Management of Property and Affairs of Mentally Incapacitated Persons" and Part IVB provides for the establishment of the Guardianship Board and the powers conferred to a guardian, which include authorization and consent to medical treatment and accommodation arrangements for mentally incapacitated persons.

I will therefore briefly introduce the roles of the Director of Social Welfare, the Official Solicitor and the Guardianship Board in the application for a Committee and a guardian under these two parts of the MHO and outline the relevant Practice Directions with which one should be familiar when making an application under Part II of the MHO.

The application procedures under Parts II and IVB of the MHO will be covered in Chapter 3.

Practice Directions

Apart from the MHO, it is important to note that the Judiciary issued Practice Direction 30.1 (**PD 30.1**) in 2005 relating to applications under Part II of the MHO. PD 30.1 covers the two-stage process of an application under Part II in detail and includes annexes with the various forms to be used in the application.

In cases where personal injuries claims are involved and the victim of a traffic accident or industrial accident becomes mentally incapacitated as a result of the acquired brain injury, provisions in Practice Direction 18.1

(**PD 18.1**)[4] relating to actions on behalf of mentally incapacitated persons will also be relevant.

Further, Order 80 of the Rules of the High Court (Cap 4A) provides that a person under disability may not make a claim in any proceedings except by his next friend (his legal representative) and may not defend any claim except by his guardian ad litem.[5] A "person under disability" is defined as a person who is a minor or a "patient". A "patient" is defined as a person who, by reason of mental disorder, is incapable of managing and administering his property and affairs within the meaning of the MHO.[6]

PD 30.1 and relevant extracts from PD 18.1 can be found at the end of this chapter.

The Role of the Director of Social Welfare

The Director of Social Welfare is the head of the Social Welfare Department which is one of the two departments under the Labour and Welfare Bureau of the Hong Kong government.

The Social Welfare Department is responsible for implementing the government's policies on social welfare including, among other things, social security, services for the elderly, family and child welfare services, medical social services and rehabilitation services for people with disabilities.

Under section 7 of the MHO, the Director of Social Welfare is given the express power to make an application to the court for an inquiry as to whether any person subject to the jurisdiction of the court who is alleged to be mentally incapacitated is, by reason of mental incapacity, incapable of managing and administering his property and affairs, if such application is not made by any relative of the person alleged to be mentally incapacitated.

The Director of Social Welfare is also given the power under section 26B of the MHO to make an application to the court in cases where no relative of the mentally incapacitated person takes action to vary any powers of a Committee already appointed or to replace the Committee with another Committee.

Additionally, the Director of Social Welfare is heavily involved in applications under Part IVB of the MHO for a Guardianship Order. Section 59N of the MHO gives power to a public officer in the Social Welfare Department to make such an application. It also expressly requires the Guardianship Board to send a copy of the application papers to the Director of Social Welfare,

---

4. Practice Direction 18.1 dated 12 February 2009, issued by the Hong Kong Judiciary.
5. Order 80 rule 2, the Rules of the High Court.
6. Order 80 rule 1, the Rules of the High Court.

unless the application is made by a public officer in the Social Welfare Department.

Furthermore, section 59P provides that the Guardianship Board must receive a social enquiry report signed by or on behalf of the Director of Social Welfare and prepared by a public officer in the Social Welfare Department for the Guardianship Board's consideration in making any Guardianship Orders.

The Director of Social Welfare may also be appointed by the Guardianship Board as a guardian under section 59S where it appears to the Guardianship Board that there is no appropriate person available to be appointed as the guardian of a mentally incapacitated person who is the subject of a guardianship application.

In the event that a private guardian appointed by the Guardianship Board dies or relinquishes the functions of a guardian, the guardianship of the mentally incapacitated person shall, subject to a review by the Guardianship Board, vest in the Director of Social Welfare.

If the private guardian is incapacitated by illness or any other cause from performing the functions of a guardian, those functions shall, during the incapacity of the guardian and subject to a review by the Guardianship Board, be performed on his behalf by the Director of Social Welfare or any other person approved by the Guardianship Board.

The Director of Social Welfare may request the Guardianship Board to review a Guardianship Order made under Part IVB of the MHO such that the Guardianship Order be varied, suspended or revoked.

The Director of Social Welfare accordingly plays a vital role, especially in relation to the guardianship applications under Part IVB of the MHO. He or she is involved in the preparation of the mandatory social enquiry report, appointed as a guardian, and empowered to make various applications to the Guardianship Board including review of any Guardianship Orders made.

For more information about the Social Welfare Department, visit its website, available at https://www.swd.gov.hk/en/index/site_dsw welcome/.

The Role of the Official Solicitor

The Official Solicitor is appointed pursuant to the Official Solicitor Ordinance (Cap 416). This Ordinance was enacted in 1991 and the Director of Legal Aid has been designated as the first Official Solicitor (**OS**). The Director of Legal Aid shall continue in effect until the Chief Executive appoints an OS.[7]

The OS is a public officer with a specific duty to look after the interest of persons under disability, eg minors under the age of 18 or adult persons with mental incapacity, in legal matters. The duties of the OS as set out under Schedule 1 to the said Ordinance include, among other things, acting as guardian ad litem or next friend to any person under a disability of age or with mental incapacity in proceedings before any court and acting as committee of the estate of a mentally incapacitated person if so appointed under the MHO.

The MHO also states that the OS can make an application to the court for an inquiry as to whether any person subject to the jurisdiction of the court who is alleged to be mentally incapacitated is, by reason of his mental incapacity, incapable of managing and administering his property and affairs under section 7 of the MHO, if such application is not made by any relative of the person alleged to be mentally incapacitated.

Similar to the Director of Social Welfare, the OS is also given the power under section 26B of the MHO to make an application to the court in cases where no relative of the mentally incapacitated person takes action to vary any powers of a Committee already appointed or to replace the Committee with another Committee, including the OS.

Under PD 30.1, notice of an application under Part II of the MHO should be given to the OS with a set of draft directions, the originating summons and relevant papers. The OS will review the papers and raise requisitions or comment on the content before the court gives a date for the inquiry.

Papers (including the draft order and skeleton bill of costs) in relation to the substantive inquiry should also be sent to the OS for comment well in advance of the inquiry.

The OS therefore plays an important role in overseeing applications made under Part II of the MHO and assisting the court by reviewing the relevant papers and providing comments. It is good practice to send papers to the OS for comments in good time to enable the OS to make observations and clarifications to an application under Part II to save time and costs at the hearing.

For more information about the Official Solicitor's Office, visit its website, available at https://www.oso.gov.hk/eng/solicitor/who.html.

---

7. See s 2 and s 7 of the Official Solicitor's Ordinance (Cap 416).

The Guardianship Board

The Guardianship Board (**Board**) is a quasi-judicial tribunal established as a body corporate under section 59J of the MHO consisting of a Chairman with legal experience, who is appointed by the Chief Executive, and not less than nine other members who shall not be public officers. The sponsoring body of the Board is the Labour and Welfare Bureau of the Hong Kong government.

Of the members of the Board, at least three shall be persons who are barristers or solicitors; at least three shall be persons who have had experience in assessing or treating mentally incapacitated persons, who may include registered medical practitioners or social workers; and at least three shall be persons other than the above two categories who have had personal experience with mentally incapacitated persons.

As mentioned earlier, Part IVB of the MHO provides for the establishment of the Board. The Board is given specific functions and powers under Part IVB of the MHO which will be discussed further in the next chapter.

The vision of the Board is to **promote the welfare, interests and protection of mentally incapacitated adults through guardianship**. To manifest its vision, the Board commits to:

1) support, protect and advocate the best interests of mentally incapacitated adults;
2) facilitate the resolution of disputes with relatives and service providers; and
3) keep the guardianship legislation under continuous review so that it promotes the best interests of mentally incapacitated adults.[8]

The values of the Board are:

1) protection;
2) compassion;
3) fairness;
4) independence;
5) respect; and
6) accessibility.

---

8. See the vision, mission and values of the Guardianship Board on its website, available at http://www.adultguardianship.org.hk/content.aspx?id=home&lang=en.

It is interesting to note that the Board has published a report, "A Case for Reform—Re-discovering Adult Guardianship",[9] which highlighted the limitations of guardianship law in Hong Kong. The Board set out key elements for reform, summarized as follows:

1) the powers of a legal guardian should be extended to include all powers as a guardian in law and equity;
2) the financial powers of a legal guardian should be extended to a Committee's powers which means the power of the Guardianship Board to appoint a Committee;
3) an independent Public Guardian and Public Trustee (Advocate) Office which can act with full Committee powers should be established; and
4) existing definitions of mentally incapacitated persons and criteria of guardianship should be replaced.

For more information on the work and services of the Guardianship Board and its vision, mission and values, visit their website: http://www.adultguardianship.org.hk/content.aspx?id=home&lang=en.

---

9. See the Guardianship Board 4th Report (2009–2011), published in 2012.

Practice Direction 30.1

Applications under
Part II of the Mental Health Ordinance (Cap. 136)

I. General

1.01 To date, there have been six judgments by Lam J on the practice and procedure for applications under Part II of the Mental Health Ordinance, Cap. 136 ("MHO"):

(a) In *Re Madam* A, HCMP No. 44 of 2004, 5 March 2004

(b) In *Re S*, HCMP No. 1287 of 2004, 28 May 2004

(c) In *Re C*, HCMP No. 424 of 2004, 7 July 2004

(d) In *Re L* [2004] 4 HKC 115

(e) In *Re LWO*, HCMP No.2965 of 2001, 30 June 2005

(f) In *Director of Social Welfare v Official Solicitor*, HCMP No.4297 of 2000, 14 September 2005

1.02 It was held in *Re Madam A* that an inquiry under Part II of the MHO involves a two-stage process: (a) the initial stage in which directions are sought from the court, ("the Directions Stage") and (b) the stage where the actual inquiry takes place ("the Inquiry Stage").

II. The Directions Stage

2.01 An Applicant should have regard to the provisions of s.7 to s.9 of the MHO in the preparation of materials to be placed before the court.

2.02 The Applicant's aim at this stage is to provide sufficient information to enable the Court to give directions for an inquiry to be held under s.10 of the MHO.

Who can apply?

2.03 Applications for an inquiry may be made by any of the parties referred to in s.7(3) of the MHO. A "relative" of the alleged mentally incapacitated person (see definition under s.2) may make the application. If there is no application by any relative, the Director of Social Welfare or the Official Solicitor or the guardian may apply.

Application for directions to be made ex parte

2.04 In general, it would be appropriate to apply ex parte for directions. Neither the alleged mentally incapacitated person nor the Official Solicitor should be named as the respondent (see *Re Madam A* paras. 8 to 15).

How to apply?

2.05 The application should follow the format of Annex A (Ex-parte Originating Summons). This format can be amended to suit the particular circumstances of any case.

2.06 The originating summons should be filed together with the supporting documents and a draft Order for directions to be given at the Directions Stage should also be lodged with the court. A return date for the hearing of the inquiry will not be given at this time. The papers will be placed before a judge for his consideration and directions. No return date will be given until the matter is ready for the hearing of the inquiry: see *Re Madam A* para.16.

All relevant & necessary information to be provided

2.07 At this stage of the application, the Applicant should ensure that there is at least prima facie evidence to justify an inquiry as to the allegation of mental incapacity.

2.08 The Applicant is duty bound to provide the court with all relevant and necessary information to enable the court to discharge its statutory duty under the MHO properly. Failure to do so will inevitably delay the application and increase the costs thereof.

2.09 The matters set out in s.7 of the MHO are the minimum requirements. In the majority of cases, the court will need much more information before it can discharge its duty properly and give appropriate and proper directions in preparation for the inquiry under s.10.

2.10 Particular regard should be paid to the matters referred to in s.7(2). The scope of the inquiry and any orders sought at the inquiry must be clearly identified at the Directions stage of the application.

2.11 The Applicant should take the precaution of canvassing the views of the alleged mentally incapacitated person and the relatives before an application is made. If the application is likely to be contested, the court must be informed of this as soon as possible. See Re S para.5.

2.12 A Certificate should accompany the application, following the format of Annex B (Certificate of Family and Property). The format can be amended to suit the particular circumstances of any case.

2.13 Where the Applicant seeks directions relating to the property and/or affairs of the alleged mentally incapacitated person, the nature and extent of his/her property as well as the number and identity of all relatives who may be affected must be made known to the court.

2.14 If the Applicant has reason to suspect or believe that the property or assets of the alleged mentally incapacitated person are being dissipated or mishandled, this should be brought to the attention of the court.

2.15 The Applicant must conduct all necessary investigations in his preparations for an application. He must ensure the adequacy of the evidence such as bank statements and medical reports. Insufficient evidence will inevitably lead to delay and the incurring of further costs.

Medical evidence

2.16 The requisite medical certificates under s.7(5) are essential (see also s. 2(2)). The medical certificates should follow the format of the specimen at Annex C (**Medical Certificate in support of an Application under Part II of the MHO**).

2.17 At least one of the medical certificates must be given by a medical practitioner approved for this purpose by the Hospital Authority within the meaning of the Hospital Authority Ordinance (Cap. 113) as having the relevant special experience (See s.2(2) of the MHO).

2.18 In order to satisfy the statutory requirements, it is essential that the medical certificates state that the alleged mentally incapacitated person is currently incapable, by reason of mental incapacity, of managing and administering his/her own property and affairs. See *Re C* paras.1 and 2.

The interests of the alleged mentally incapacitated person are paramount

2.19 In seeking directions, the Applicant must bear in mind that the interests and requirements of the alleged mentally incapacitated person are paramount see s.10A(2)(a). For instance the court will have regard to the existing and future care arrangements for the alleged mentally incapacitated person; the costs thereof; the health condition of the alleged mentally incapacitated person; his life expectancy; the maintenance of the family members of the alleged mentally incapacitated person; the income and expenditure of the family of the alleged mentally incapacitated person and other matters. See *Re S* para.3.

Application for appointment of a committee of estate (s.11 of MHO)

2.20 Where the appointment of a committee of the estate of an alleged mentally incapacitated person is sought, the court must be provided with all relevant and necessary information regarding the members of the proposed committee. Information as to the background, training, qualification and experience of members of the committee must be provided, as well as the manner in which the Applicant envisages how the proposed committee will manage and administer the property and affairs of the alleged mentally incapacitated person. For the form of Consent to Appointment as Committee, see Annex D.

Notice to the Official Solicitor

2.21 Notice of the application should be given to the Official Solicitor. The Applicant should submit a set of draft directions together with the Originating Summons and other documents to the Official Solicitor.

Paper applications

2.22 Normally, directions will be given after consideration on the papers without a hearing unless the court considers, whether upon request or on the court's own motion, that a hearing should be held. Such a request should be made in writing at the time of the filing of the Originating Summons.

Notice of the Inquiry must be served on the alleged mentally incapacitated person

2.23 Notice of the inquiry must be served on the alleged mentally incapacitated person. Such Notice cannot be dispensed with. See *Re Madam A* paras.25 and 26.

2.24 In the application, the Applicant must indicate to the court the appropriate mode of service on the alleged mentally incapacitated person. Furthermore, the alleged mentally incapacitated person must be given reasonable notice of the time and place of the inquiry normally by personal service: see s.8 of the MHO. It is only if the alleged mentally incapacitated person is in such a state that personal service on him would be ineffectual that substituted service falls to be considered.

2.25 Substituted service in this context is not by way of advertisement in a newspaper: see *Re Madam A* para.25. Substituted service by way of serving the notice on the person in charge of the institution having the care of the alleged mentally incapacitated person may be considered.

Urgency

2.26 In cases of urgency the Applicant may consider an application under s.10D and/or s.10A(1), see *Re L*.

Estates without substantial assets

2.27 In cases where the estates do not involve substantial assets an order under s.24 should be considered.

Draft Order

2.28 Solicitors for the Applicant must ensure that the draft order contains all the directions to be sought in the s.7 application. The draft order should be lodged at the time of the filing of the application and should follow the format of the specimen at Annex E.

2.29 The proposed directions should generally deal with the following matters:

    (a) a clear indication of the scope of the inquiry, e.g. appointment of a committee;

(b) a list of the persons to be served with Notice of the inquiry;

(c) the mode of service of the Notice on the alleged mentally incapacitated person, and whether it should be by way of substituted service, and if so, why;

(d) whether further evidence will be required or adduced at the inquiry;

(e) whether it is proposed that a medical examination be conducted;

(f) whether it will be necessary to identify and/or trace relatives or next of kin;

(g) proposed directions covering all aspects relating to the property and affairs of the alleged mentally incapacitated person;

(h) whether the doctors who compiled the reports should attend the inquiry;

(i) whether any interim relief is necessary, or any interim directions should be issued for the protection of the property of the alleged mentally incapacitated person;

(j) an estimate of the length of the inquiry.

III. The Inquiry Stage

3.01 A draft order containing all the reliefs sought in the s.10 hearing must be submitted to the court. A draft order (which should follow the format of the specimen at Annex F) and skeleton bill of costs (if intended to be paid out of the estate of the mentally incapacitated person) shall be lodged with the court at least 10 clear days before hearing (Saturdays, Sundays and public holidays excluded). The court will usually fix the costs pursuant to Order 62 Rule 9(4)(b) instead of directing taxation in order to save costs.

3.02 Given the role of the Official Solicitor, applicants should send a set of papers to the Official Solicitor for comment well in advance of the inquiry.

3.03 At the inquiry, the court will consider and decide on those matters referred to in s.10 of the MHO.

3.04 At the inquiry, the Court may appoint a committee of the estate of the alleged mentally incapacitated person if it is satisfied that the person is, by reason of mental incapacity, incapable of managing and administering his property and affairs: see s.11.

3.05 The court may also direct the sale of any property of the mentally incapacitated person under s.10A and s.10B of the MHO. If this is contemplated, the application should be supported by proper valuation evidence. The draft order should also contain appropriate directions as to conduct of the sale and the distribution or disposal of sale proceeds.

IV. Further Directions after Appointment of Committee

4.01 From time to time a Committee of the estate appointed by the court may have to report to or seek directions from the court pursuant to section 13 or other provisions of the Ordinance.

4.02 Such reports or applications should be filed with court at the High Court Registry. Sending the documents by mail or simply lodging them at the Reception Counter of the High Court Registry does not comply with the duty to file under this paragraph.

4.03 When reports, applications, accounts or other documents are filed in the post-inquiry period, it is essential to state on the top of the first page of the document that it must be brought to the attention of the Judge or the Registrar as appropriate. Failure to do so may result in delay and inconvenience. Words to the effect that the document is "*For the attention of the Judge/Registrar*" will ensure that the document reaches the Judge or Registrar as early as possible.

4.04 Consideration could be given for the discharge of the committee after the more complicated steps in the administration and management of the estate have been completed and thereafter properties could be dealt with by a less costly alternative like an order under s.24, see *Director of Social Welfare v Official Solicitor*.

V. Personal Injuries Cases

5.01 In the handling of personal injuries cases in which an injured person who has been granted or who is seeking compensation may fall within the meaning of "a mentally incapacitated person" of the MHO, consideration should be given to whether an application under Part II of the MHO should be made, see *Re LWO*.

5.02 Where it is considered necessary for the Plaintiff to apply for a committee to be appointed, this should be brought to the notice of the judge hearing the PI claim. The compensation may include the costs of a Part II application.

VI. Miscellaneous

6.01 Applicants should exercise their own judgment as to whether they could simply adopt the forms included in the Annexures, or to make any modifications to the same as the circumstances of the case may require.

6.02 Applications under Part II of the Mental Health Ordinance fall within the same category as those set out in Paragraph 4 of PD25.1 and hearings are usually not open to the public.

6.03 This Practice Direction will come into effect on 31 October 2005.

Dated this 10th day of October 2005.

Andrew Li
Chief Justice

ANNEX A

ANNEX B

ANNEX C

ANNEX D

ANNEX E

ANNEX F

Extract from Practice Direction—18.1
The Personal Injuries List

1. This Practice Direction identifies and gives effect to the relevant changes in civil procedure introduced by the Rules of High Court (Amendment) Rules 2008 which came into effect on 2 April 2009.

2. The Practice Direction is issued for the guidance of practitioners involved in personal injury matters. It is not a substitute for detailed knowledge of the relevant Rules of the High Court ("RHC") (Cap 4A). It is imperative that practitioners should keep themselves abreast of the changes brought about by the Civil Justice Reform and familiarize themselves with the Rules of the Court implementing the Civil Justice Reform, especially the underlying objectives and the Court's case management powers under RHC, Orders 1A and 1B.

X Actions by Persons under Disability

182. RHC, Order 80, rule 3 sets out carefully the considerations for the appointment of the next friend or guardian. A divorced wife is not to be regarded as appropriate. Such a person is unlikely to meet the requirement of RHC, Order 80, rule 3(8)(c)(iii).

183. RHC, Order 80, rules 10, 11 and 12 will be strictly applied. It is improper to seek a Consent Order under RHC, Order 42, rule 5A for settlement of an action by a person under disability and practitioners should in no circumstances attempt to do so.

184. Claims under the Fatal Accidents Ordinance (Cap 22) and the Law Amendment and Reform (Consolidation) Ordinance (Cap 23) which include claims on behalf of an infant dependant, or a dependant under any other disability, require approval by the Court of any proposed settlement.

185. Practitioners are required to follow the procedure set out in the Hong Kong Civil Procedure 2009 paragraphs 80/11/8 to 80/11/9 at pages 1166 to 1167.

186. In any application to the Court for approval for settlement of an action involving a person under disability, or for payment out of sums paid into Court for the benefit of a person under disability and / or for variation of Court orders relating to payment out of such sums, Solicitors acting for the person under disability must ensure that the Memorandum in support of the application prepared by the Solicitor having prime responsibility for the action must contain full details of all relevant matters to enable the Court to consider the matter fully, including, without limitation, the following:

(1) whether there is any corresponding EC Action and / or other litigation involving the person under disability;

(2) if so, state in relation to such EC Action or other litigation the action number and the names of the parties and their Solicitors (if any);

(3) whether any sums have been awarded or agreed to be paid (whether on interim or final basis) in favour of the person under disability in such other cases, with copies of the relevant Court orders;

(4) if so, whether such sums have been paid into Court or whether there are any or any other Suitors' Funds held by the District Court and / or the High Court for the benefit of the person under disability; and

(5) whether any sums (whether by lump sum, periodical or other mode of payment) have been or will be paid out of Court with copies of the relevant Court orders.

187. At the hearing of the application for approval of any compromise or settlement, the Plaintiff's Solicitors are required to set out all proposed directions as to the disposal of any of the monies which form a part of such compromise or settlement. The contents of the Order sought should follow Form PF 170 or PF 171, as appropriate, at pages 114/115 of Volume 2 of The Supreme Court Practice 1999.

188. In respect of a person under disability by reason of mental incapacity, practitioners should be mindful of the jurisdiction of the High Court under Part II of the Mental Health Ordinance (Cap 136) ("MHO") and the practice set out under Part Y hereof. Solicitors are expected to advise their clients (both the person under disability as well as his next friend and other relatives) about the same before the commencement of legal proceedings, during the course of the proceedings as well as after judgment is entered and / or settlement is achieved.

189. Save as is otherwise ordered by the Judge the proper order for costs in respect of such compromised proceedings is on a common fund basis.

190. In the event of a Solicitor for a Plaintiff seeking to charge against a Plaintiff's damages, costs and disbursements which he considers he will not recover from the Defendant(s), he must produce at the hearing for approval a statement of the maximum amount of such costs and disbursements and will be required to justify them. The Plaintiff and / or the next friend must have been advised in writing of the estimate of the amount of costs and disbursements in question, and any consent thereto must be in writing and produced to the Court. The written advice must set out clearly why those costs and disbursements have been incurred and why it is considered that they are not recoverable from the Defendant(s). A general undertaking to be responsible for costs signed by the client will not be sufficient for these purposes.

The proposed direction set out by the Plaintiff's Solicitors pursuant to paragraph 187 hereof should also set out how the balance of the amount of such costs and disbursements after deduction of the taxed costs payable to them should be settled by or on behalf of the Plaintiff.

No approval will be given to any settlement unless the Court can be told with reasonable accuracy, the maximum amount it is sought to be deducted from the Plaintiff's damages. If the Court is not satisfied with the maximum amount as put forward by the Plaintiff's Solicitors as being necessary, the Court may, whilst granting an approval of the settlement figure, give such directions for dealing with the application for approval of the distribution of the award as it thinks fit, including a speedy taxation of all the costs and disbursements.

191. No amount of damages will be released from the Court's control and investment on behalf of a claimant, save for direct transmission to the claimant e.g. for the benefit of the widow and family in a fatal claim, until it is satisfied that any claim for costs and disbursements as set out in paragraph 190 hereof and / or by virtue of the First Charge of the Director of Legal Aid has been quantified.

192. If, after the Order 80 approval, it becomes apparent that a Plaintiff who is under disability will have to pay costs in an amount higher than the amount stated at the Order 80 hearing, the Plaintiff's Solicitors should immediately inform the Court with full details of the reasons and seek directions. The Court will not entertain such application unless the Plaintiff is properly represented and his interest is sufficiently protected.

Y Part II of MHO

193.

(1) Practitioners acting for a mentally incapacitated person ("MIP") on instructions from a next friend should bear in mind their duties towards the MIP and give consideration to the appointment of a committee or seeking other directions under Part II of the MHO. Relevant guidance is set out in Re CK, HCMP 1150 of 2006 and Re YPC, HCMP 1174 of 2006.

(2) Solicitors acting for an MIP who has been a breadwinner for his / her family should take specific instructions regarding the means of support for the family after the accident. If loans were raised for that purpose, an application under Part II of the MHO should be made to avoid the difficulties in Re YWK HCMP 2467 of 2006 and Re C HCMP 15 of 2002.

(3) Practitioners are reminded that after an appointment of committee under Part II of the MHO, nobody else apart from the committee should be permitted to act as the next friend of an MIP to pursue a claim for the MIP unless the Court otherwise orders.

194. A committee should apply for specific authorization under Part II of the MHO to commence or defend legal proceedings. Such application should be supported by evidence as to the following:

(1) the merits of the intended claim;

(2) the benefit that the MIP might derive from the intended claim;

(3) the estimate costs of prosecuting the claim;

(4) the resource available to meet such costs;

(5) the alternative options including alternative modes of dispute resolution that may achieve similar benefit for the MIP; and

(6) the exposure of the estate of the MIP to costs liability of the opposite party in case the action fails.

Z Approval of Settlement under RHC, Order 80 involving an MIP

195. Where Part II proceedings have not been commenced before settlement, the Court may direct such proceedings to be commenced in the course of approval of settlement. In considering whether Part II proceedings should be required when approving a settlement under RHC, Order 80 involving an MIP, the Court will exercise its discretion by reference to what is in the best interest of that particular MIP in the context of the factual matrix of the case before the Court. The following factors can be relevant:

(1) the condition of the MIP including his or her age and prognosis;

(2) the future needs and requirements of the MIP;

(3) the quantum of the award and, without prejudice to the Court's discretion to direct proceedings under Part II of the MHO to be commenced in respect of the particular case before the Court, the appointment of a committee will generally not be necessary when the award, and where the particular MIP is involved in more than one action, the accumulated awards, is / are not more than HK$1 million or such sum as the Court may direct from time to time;

(4) the background and experience of the next friend including the relationship of the next friend with the MIP and the ability of the next friend to keep proper account and to appreciate his duty;

(5) the adequacy of advice regarding the duty of a next friend;

(6) the needs and resources of the MIP's family;

(7) the likelihood of applications to use funds in Court for acquisitions of a capital nature;

(8) the attitude of the primary carer of the MIP and, to a lesser extent, the attitude of the immediate family members of the MIP; and

(9) the possible alternatives in terms of investment of the funds as opposed to leaving the monies in Court.

196. If the Court comes to the conclusion that Part II proceedings should be instituted to protect the interest of the MIP but the proceedings have yet to be commenced, approval for settlement may still be obtained under RHC, Order 80 provided that the terms to be approved under RHC, Order 80 should provide for the following:

(1) for once and for all payment out (if any) like disbursement of legal expenses or reimbursement of money previously spent on maintenance of the

MIP and / or periodic payment out for maintenance of the MIP (if any), the PI Judge or PI Master can deal with the same under RHC, Order 80, rule 12;

(2) the balance of the funds shall remain in Court pending Part II proceedings; and

(3) the disposal of the balance of the funds in Court shall be in accordance with the directions of the Court in the Part II proceedings.

197. Where a committee has been set up before settlement, the committee shall file an application in the context of the Part II proceedings for sanctioning the settlement in which the committee was appointed and the papers will be passed to the Registrar of the High Court for a report under section 13 of the MHO. Based on the report of the Registrar, the Court will usually deal with the application on paper. A hearing will only be required if the Court so directs. The committee should only apply for approval pursuant to RHC, Order 80 after it has obtained sanction under Part II of the MHO. The committee should also draw the Court's attention to the Part II approval in the Order 80 application.

198. For cases where the Court does not require Part II proceedings to be taken out and orders payment out from the Suitors' Fund on a periodical basis or otherwise for the maintenance or benefit of the MIP, Solicitors acting for the MIP should advise the recipient of the periodical payments as regards the following:

(1) the money is to be paid to the recipient for the maintenance and benefit of the MIP and not for any other purposes;

(2) the recipient should keep account of monies paid to him / her and upon request by the Court, he / she should be ready to produce such account for inspection;

(3) if the Court pays out a sum for a specific purpose, it should not be used for other purposes without any prior approval from th Court;

(4) the recipient has a duty to inform the Master in charge of Suitors' Fund of any material change of circumstances including reduction or increase in expenditure for the maintenance of the MIP, recovery or deterioration of the MIP, accumulation of surplus from monies paid out, changes in the relationship between the MIP and the recipient, and changes in the needs of the MIP.

199. The Court may require assurance from the Solicitor acting for the MIP that the above advice has been given and undertakings from the recipient to comply with paragraphs 198(1) to 198(4) hereof.

AA Minors

200. Solicitors acting for minors are reminded that paragraph 198 hereof will apply with suitable adaptations to minors as for MIPs.

3
Committee versus Guardian

I have set out a brief overview of the Mental Health Ordinance (Cap 136) (**MHO**) in Chapter 2. Since this book is written mainly for family members and carers of the elderly and special needs persons, the focus in this chapter will be on Parts II and IVB of the MHO which concern the management of finances and property as well as the accommodation and care arrangements for these persons.

I will highlight the difference between a Committee and a guardian in this chapter and walk you through the application process for the appointment of a Committee (commonly referred to as "**Part II application under the MHO**") and a guardian (commonly referred to as "**Part IVB application under the MHO**").

The Committee of the estate of a mentally incapacitated person (commonly referred to as an "**MIP**"), when appointed by the court, has statutory power to manage the finances and property of the MIP. The guardian, when appointed by the Guardianship Board, has statutory power to make decisions on accommodation and care arrangements for the MIP.

Appointment of a Committee

I. When is it necessary to make a Part II application under the MHO?

When a person is assessed to be mentally incapable of managing his or her property and affairs, ie an MIP, he or she will need someone to help manage and administer his or her finances and financial affairs, such as bank accounts, stocks and investments, signing or renewing rental agreements, buying and selling properties, settling bank mortgages, management fees, utility bills, tax and other payments, etc. Thus, the appointment of a Committee for the MIP may be necessary.

Such MIPs, in addition to requiring help in the management of their finances, may also have difficulty in self-care and lack the ability to decide on what medical treatment or accommodation needs are necessary and appropriate. Hence there may be a concurrent need to appoint a guardian under Part IVB of the MHO for the MIP, especially when there are disputes between the MIP's family members on these matters.

You will note in the latter part of this chapter that a guardian, while having the power to look after the medical and other needs of such persons, only has limited power to settle hospital bills and make payments up to HK$17,000 per month.[1]

Some examples of the circumstances where it may be necessary to take out a Part II application are as follows:

> 1) where the MIP as a landlord has a landed property rented out to a tenant who refuses to pay rent, when the MIP is hospitalized or suffering from some form of brain injury rendering him mentally incapable of managing his property and affairs, a Committee may need to be appointed to issue recovery proceedings against the tenant in addition to the usual scope and powers;
> 2) where substantial sums of money have been withdrawn from the MIP's bank account or there are suspicious transactions or improper dealings with the MIP's assets requiring investigation or issuance of legal proceedings against a third party, it may be necessary to appoint a Committee; and
> 3) where a person has signed a preliminary agreement to buy or sell a landed property but becomes an MIP before completion, it may be necessary to take out an Emergency Order under Part II of the MHO to appoint a Committee with the specific power to sign and seal all documents relating to the purchase or sale of the property, etc.

On the other hand, if the MIP has minimal or no assets that require to be managed, there may not be a need for a Part II application.

II. Who can apply for the appointment of a Committee?

Part II of the MHO provides for the management of the property and affairs of elderly and special needs persons who have been assessed to be mentally incapable of handling their financial affairs (also commonly referred to as MIPs).

---

1. See the "Monthly Financial Limit" of a guardian dated 30 November 2018 on the Guardianship Board's website.

So, who can initiate or apply for the appointment of a Committee?

Most commonly, a relative or next of kin of the person alleged to be mentally incapacitated may make an application to the court for an order that the person is indeed, by reason of mental incapacity, incapable of managing his or her own property and affairs. On some occasions, it may be necessary for the Director of Social Welfare, Official Solicitor or guardian to make such application to protect a person from potential or actual financial abuse.

The Mental Health Court of the High Court of Hong Kong will hear applications made by family members as well as applications made by the Director of Social Welfare, the Official Solicitor or the guardian for a Committee to be appointed on behalf of an MIP as necessary and appropriate.

III. *The application procedure*

The application procedure is generally set out in PD30.1, as set out in the previous chapter. In gist, it is a two-stage process with the first stage being a *Directions Stage* and the second stage being the *Inquiry Stage*. This does not mean that there will be two separate court hearings, as the first stage can usually be dealt with on paper.

Here is a summary of the Part II application for a Committee to be appointed for an MIP:

1. Who can apply?

> The following persons may apply for a Committee to be appointed:
> a. relatives of the MIP
> b. the Director of Social Welfare
> c. the Official Solicitor
> d. guardian appointed under Part IVB of the MHO

2. How to apply?

The first stage: Ex-parte application[2]

> The application (which is referred to as an "**Ex-parte Originating Summons**") should be accompanied by the following documents:
> a. a Certificate of Family and Property;

---

2. See s 7(3) of the MHO. The first stage is an ex-parte application which means that it is made by one party to the application only, not between two parties or more.

> b. medical evidence, ie two medical certificates;[3]
> c. Consent to Act by the proposed Committee; and
> d. a Draft Order for directions.

The court upon receiving the application may give directions for the Inquiry (**Notice of Inquiry**) and the applicant will have to submit the draft order for substantive relief and skeleton bill of costs. If the costs of the application are to be paid out from the estate of the MIP,[4] a copy of all the papers must be submitted to the Official Solicitor's Office for his comments. The Notice of Inquiry must be served on the MIP and all relevant parties including the Official Solicitor as directed by the court.

3. The Inquiry

The second stage: Inquiry hearing

At the Inquiry hearing, the court will hear submissions from the applicant doctors (unless attendance has been dispensed with) and any opposing parties before deciding whether or not the alleged MIP is incapable of managing and administering his property and affairs.

The court, once satisfied that a Committee should be appointed for the alleged MIP, will make such specific orders as necessary to empower the Committee to manage and administer the MIP's assets efficiently and appropriately.

The court will also order the Committee to prepare annual accounts in relation to the MIP's financial position. A standard draft order detailing all the outcomes to be sought at the hearing can be found in Annex F of PD30.1.

IV. Duties of the Committee

The Committee's duties are set out in the court orders and any subsequent directions made, which may include the following:[5]

> 1) opening the Committee's bank accounts and safe deposit boxes on behalf of the MIP;
> 2) withdrawal of the MIP's money and shares in banks and transferring them into the Committee's bank account;

---

3. Two medical certificates, one of which must be from an approved doctor under s 2(2) of the MHO. A list of approved doctors can be downloaded from the Board's website, available at http://www.adultguardianship.org.hk/admin/Data/uploadfile/174/L2Erev4.pdf.
4. See PD30.1 and the cases of Re A and Re C referred to in PD30.1.
5. See "Guidance Note to Persons Appointed as Committee of a Mentally Incapacitated Person", published by the Hong Kong Judiciary.

3) payment of the MIP's maintenance and expenses including any debts of the MIP;
4) taking possession of wills and codicils; and
5) taking steps to ascertain and verify the MIP's assets in Hong Kong or elsewhere.

V. Powers of the Court

The Court has power to make orders involving the MIP's assets including:

1) sale, exchange or other disposition of property (including business premises);
2) acquisition and settlement of property (including gifts to other persons);[6]
3) execution of statutory wills;
4) carrying on of trade or business;
5) dissolution of partnership of which the MIP is a member;
6) carrying out of any contract entered into by the MIP;
7) conducting legal proceedings in the name of the MIP; and
8) orders that could have been made under the Trustee Ordinance (Cap 29).

It is important to note that Part II applications are different from ordinary adversarial civil litigation since the court is exercising a protective jurisdiction over the property and affairs of the MIP. It is not a forum for large and complex disputes between family members. The court usually focuses on whether a person is an MIP and, if so, whether it is appropriate to appoint a Committee to protect the MIP.

In considering the suitability of persons to be appointed as the Committee of the MIP, the court traditionally prefers family members and relatives to strangers. This is not only because relatives are willing to act without remuneration, but also because they are most familiar with the MIP and should be in a better position to manage the property and affairs of the MIP.

However, sometimes there may be a dispute between family members and relatives as to who is the more appropriate person to be appointed as the Committee of the MIP. The court will in appropriate circumstances appoint an independent person such as an accountant, solicitor or, as a last resort, the Official Solicitor.

---

6. See s 10A(1)(b) or (c) of the MHO.

Appointment of a Guardian

I. When is it necessary to apply for a Guardianship Order?

In most cases, it will *not* be necessary to apply for a Guardianship Order. If the MIP has the capacity to consent, he or she should be entitled to make his or her own decision on medical treatment.

If the MIP is unable to give consent to receiving a medical treatment, the doctor can provide non-urgent medical treatment, which is necessary and in the MIP's best interests, without his or her consent. This is only applicable where the doctor has taken all reasonably practicable steps to ascertain whether a legal guardian has been appointed and there appears to be no guardian appointed.[7]

However, if a family member objects to the treatment that is in the best interests of the MIP, another family member, social worker or treating doctor who wishes to protect the interests of the MIP's welfare should apply to the Guardianship Board to have a guardian appointed.

Also, if an MIP strongly refuses or resists a treatment that is in his or her best interests, a family member, social worker or treating doctor who wishes to protect the interests of the MIP's welfare should apply to the Board to have a guardian appointed.

If a private guardian (as opposed to the Director of Social Welfare, who is referred to as the "**Public Guardian**") is appointed, he or she is authorized to make decisions with the powers he or she has been granted in the order. If the Director of Social Welfare is appointed, a public officer acting on behalf of the Director of Social Welfare will begin to make decisions with the powers given in that order.

II. Who appoints a guardian?

The Guardianship Board operating under Part IVB of the MHO will conduct hearings and appoint a guardian under Guardianship Orders for any person aged 18 years or above with decision making incapacities (**Person Concerned**) so as to promote and protect the Person Concerned's interests.

If the Person Concerned can no longer make reasonable decisions regarding his own welfare and personal circumstances, he may be assessed by an approved doctor[8] to be an MIP.

In the following paragraphs, a Person Concerned refers to a person who is suspected to lack the ability to make reasonable decisions regarding his own welfare and personal circumstances, and an MIP refers to a person who

---

7. Section 59ZF(2) and (3) of the MHO.
8. Section 2(2) of the MHO.

has been assessed by an approved doctor to lack the mental capacity to make such decisions.

Once the Person Concerned is assessed to be an MIP, a private guardian, ie a family member or friend, or the Public Guardian may be appointed as the guardian of the MIP.

The guardian appointed by the Guardianship Board may have such powers as specified in the Guardianship Order[9] summarized below (commonly referred to as the "**six powers of the Guardian**"):

> 1) to specify and arrange for the MIP's residence;
> 2) to bring the MIP to a specific place as necessary;
> 3) to bring the MIP to attend medical and other treatments or training;
> 4) to consent to medical or dental treatment on behalf of the MIP;
> 5) to facilitate access to the MIP by any doctor, approved social worker or other persons specified in the Guardianship Order; and
> 6) to keep a monthly sum of HK$17,000[10] for the maintenance or benefit of the MIP.

The Guardianship Board may, if it is satisfied that the Person Concerned is in need of a guardian after a) conducting a hearing on any guardianship application for the purpose of determining whether the Person Concerned should be received into guardianship and having regard to the representations (if any) of any person present at the hearing; and b) considering the social enquiry report, make an order appointing a guardian in respect of that person.[11]

In considering whether or not to make a Guardianship Order, the Guardianship Board should consider the interests of the Person Concerned, and if the Board concludes that it is in the interest of the Person Concerned to override the views and wishes of the Person Concerned, it may do so.[12]

Three of the criteria when considering the merits of a guardianship application should be highlighted:

> 1) the Person Concerned is suffering from a form of mental disorder or mental handicap that limits him or her in making reasonable

---

9. Section 59R(3) of the MHO.
10. See s 59R(3)(f) and s 44B(8) of the MHO. The monthly sum does not exceed the latest median monthly employment earnings of employed persons specified in the "Quarterly Report on General Household Survey" published by the Census and Statistics Department.
11. See s 59O(1) of the MHO.
12. See s 59K(2) of the MHO.

> decisions in respect of all or a substantial proportion of the matters which relate to his or her personal circumstances;
> 2) the particular needs of the Person Concerned may only be met or attended to by his being received into guardianship under Part IVB of the MHO; and
> 3) no other less restrictive or intrusive means are available in the circumstances and it is in the interests of the welfare of the Person Concerned or for the protection of other persons to receive the Person Concerned into guardianship.[13]

Any Guardianship Order made shall be subject to such terms and conditions as the Guardianship Board thinks fit, including terms and conditions (if any) as to the exercise, extent and duration of any particular powers and duties of the guardian.[14]

I. Application procedure for a Guardianship Order

1. Preparation for application

The applicant must file an application in the prescribed form and obtain two medical reports on the Person Concerned in the prescribed form.[15]

2. Submission of Form 1 and medical reports

The applicant should submit the application Form 1 and two medical reports within 14 days after the applicant has last seen the Person Concerned. The two medical reports must be sent to the Guardianship Board within 14 days of the last medical examination of the Person Concerned. One of the reports must be prepared by an approved doctor, ie a doctor with special experience in diagnosing, treating and assessing or determining mental disorder.

3. Request for social enquiry report

The Guardianship Board's secretariat will check the Form 1 and two medical reports to ensure that they are properly completed. Thereafter the application will be processed and a copy of the Form 1 and two medical reports will be sent to the Director of Social Welfare.

The Board must then request the Social Welfare Department to prepare a social enquiry report on the Concerned Person and his or her family within

---

13. See s 59O(3)(b) to (d) of the MHO.
14. See s 59O(2) of the MHO.
15. Refer to PD30.1 for the sample Form 1 and medical reports in the prescribed format.

four weeks. The social worker assigned to prepare the report will interview the applicant and the Person Concerned to ascertain their views and wishes.

4. Date, time, and venue for hearing

When all the documents are in order and the social enquiry report has been filed with the Board, the secretariat will arrange a date for the hearing and notify the applicant, the Person Concerned, the Director of Social Welfare as well as the proposed guardian and other relevant persons such as relatives, doctors, social workers and carers as appropriate, giving the parties two weeks' notice of the hearing date.

Processing time is generally three to nine months from the date of receipt of a duly completed Form 1 until the actual hearing.

5. The hearing

The Board will assess the medical reports, social enquiry report and oral information given at the hearing before making an order for the appointment of a guardian.

The hearing normally lasts for 20 to 45 minutes. At least three Board members hear a case. They will consider the relevant written evidence and take oral evidence from those attending the hearing. The Board may also allow some witnesses to give evidence over the telephone. After considering the evidence as a whole, the Board will make decision if a guardian is required and, if so, who it will be and what powers the guardian will have.

6. The Guardianship Order

The Board gives written orders together with reasons which are sent out to parties within seven days after the hearing.

A social worker of the Social Welfare Department will be assigned to follow up each guardianship case until the order is discharged. The private guardian must fully cooperate with the case social worker and provide all relevant information including accommodation, finances and medical treatment to the case social worker during the period of the order. The case social worker will visit the subject each month and the guardian should have regular meetings and keep contact with the case social worker and provide reports every month including monthly accounts and all relevant information.

Where a subject dies whilst under guardianship, a coroner shall hold an inquest into the death. The guardian should notify the Director of Social Welfare no later than 14 days after the subject's death, report the death to the coroner via the Commissioner of Police, and immediately inform the hospital of the subject's guardianship status in order that the funeral can be arranged smoothly.

Any party to proceedings before the Guardianship Board may appeal to the court after any decision of the Board on a question of law or with the leave of the court on any other question.[16]

It should be noted that the Guardianship Board may of its own initiative review any Guardianship Order with a view to varying, suspending or revoking the Guardianship Order in the interest and welfare of the person received into guardianship.[17]

Table 3.1: Comparison of Guardian and Committee

	Guardian (Part IVB of the MHO)	**Committee (Part II of the MHO)**
Order	The Guardianship Board, on application, may appoint a person to be a guardian of an MIP who is **18 or above** and **is in need of a guardian,** ie having considered whether the MIP can make reasonable decisions on his personal circumstances, his particular needs, interest and welfare, etc (section 59O).	The Court of First Instance may appoint a Committee of the estate of an MIP, if it is satisfied that the person who is alleged to be mentally incapacitated is, **by reason of mental incapacity, incapable of** managing and administering his property and affairs (section 11). The Court may make orders directing inquiry as to whether any person who is alleged to be mentally incapacitated is, by reason of mental incapacity, incapable of managing and administering his property and affairs (sections 7–10).
When and why	In most cases, it may not be necessary to apply for a Guardianship Order for an elderly person or persons with special needs. However, when a person is suffering from mental disorder or handicap rendering that person unable to make reasonable decisions in respect of all or a substantial portion of the matters relating to his or her personal circumstances, in the absence of	When a person is assessed to be mentally incapacitated and requires someone to help manage and administer his or her finances, such as bank accounts, stocks and investments, signing and renewing rental agreements, buying and selling property, settling bills, etc, or when there is suspicion of financial abuse, appointment of a Committee may be necessary.

(continued on page 47)

---

16. See s 59W of the MHO.
17. See s 59U of the MHO.

Table 3.1 (continued)

	Guardian (Part IVB of the MHO)	**Committee (Part II of the MHO)**
	less restrictive or intrusive means available, it may be necessary and in his or her best interests to receive that person into guardianship.	
Term	Initial order is up to one year (section 59R(1)). Upon review, it can be made for up to three years (section 59R(1)). An Emergency Order can be made for up to three months (section 59R(2)).	It is discharged by court order on the court being satisfied that the MIP has become capable of managing and administering his or her property and affairs, by court order at any time, or upon the MIP's death (section 27(4)).
Duties	The guardian has duty to act in the best interests of the MIP at all times. Private guardians also owe duties to permit access to the MIP, and to inform the Director of Social Welfare regarding any changes of circumstances of the MIP (see Regulation 3 of the Mental Health (Guardianship) Regulations, Cap 136D). This is subject to review by the Guardianship Board (section 59U).	The Committee has duty to act in the best interests of the MIP at all times. The Committee also owes duties to the court, eg to inform the court about any changes in the MIP's financial situation, recovery, death, etc.*
Powers	Scope of power, including terms and conditions, is defined in the Guardianship Order (section 59O). Eg: The guardian is allowed to hold, receive or pay a specified sum up to a maximum of HK$17,000 per month.‡	Scope of power is defined in the Committee Order or by court direction, as conferred by the court under sections 10A and 10B (sections 11–12).

(continued on page 48)

Notes:
* See "Guidance Note to Persons appointed as Committee of Estate of a Mentally Incapacitated Person", issued by the Hong Kong Judiciary.
‡ As of 30 November 2018. See s 59R(3)(f) and s 44B(8) of the MHO.

Table 3.1 (continued)

	Guardian (Part IVB of the MHO)	Committee (Part II of the MHO)
	Eg: The guardian has power to authorize or consent to any medical or dental treatment, or to make any decision regarding the residence of the MIP (section 59R(3)(a), (d)).	The Committee has wider power to manage and administer the property of an MIP, eg sale and settlement of the MIP's properties, conducting legal proceedings, and executing wills (see sections 10A, 10B & 21–23). It has no power to authorize or consent to medical or dental treatment or make any decision regarding the MIP's residence.

Figure 3.1: Guardian vs Committee

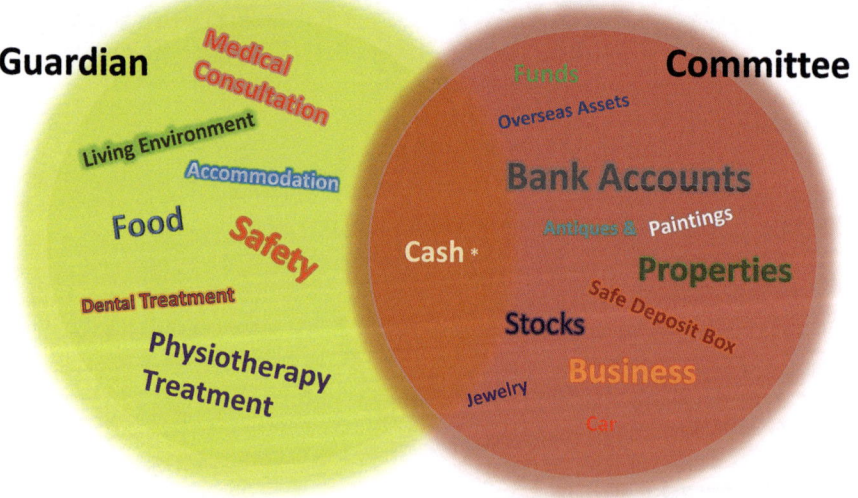

* A Guardian is allowed to hold, receive or pay a sum up to HK$17,000 per month, which is based on the median monthly employment earnings specified in the Quarterly Report on General Household Survey published by the Census and Statistics Department, currently adjusted to HK$17,000 (as of 30 November 2018).

Figure 3.2: Procedures on Appointment of Guardian and Committee

Part IVB MHO*
Appointment of Guardian
(to authorize or consent to any medical/ dental treatment, and accommodation of the MIP**)

Potential applicants
(i) Relative
(ii) Social worker
(iii) Registered medical practitioner
(iv) Director of Social Welfare

1st stage: Prepare necessary documents
(i) Form 1: Application form for Guardianship Order
(ii) Two written reports prepared by registered medical practitioners

2nd stage: Upon receiving an application, the Guardianship Board will:
1. Send copies of the application to the alleged MIP, relative of the alleged MIP, and the Director of Social Welfare (as appropriate)
2. Director of Social Welfare to prepare a social enquiry report (3-9 weeks)
3. Fix date for hearing

3rd stage: Guardianship Board Hearing

Part II MHO*
Appointment of Committee
(e.g. to manage the financial property and affairs of the MIP**)

Potential applicants
(i) Relative
(ii) Director of Social Welfare
(iii) Official Solicitor
(iv) Guardian of the alleged MIP

1st stage: Ex-parte application
Documents required:
(i) Two medical certificates
(ii) Certificate of Family and Property
(iii) Consent to Act by the proposed Committee
(iv) Draft Order for directions
Documents to be served on Official Solicitor

2nd stage: Inquiry
(a) Directions stage (Without hearing)
- Notice of inquiry served on the alleged MIP, Official Solicitor and other related parties as directed by Court

(b) 10 clear days before the Inquiry hearing
- Draft order containing all necessary directions (e.g. mode of service, scope of inquiry, any interim relief)
- Skeleton bill of costs

(c) Inquiry hearing
- Decide whether the alleged MIP is incapable of managing and administering his property and affairs
- Make substantive order

*Mental Health Ordinance (Cap. 136)
**Mentally incapacitated person

4
Mental Capacity

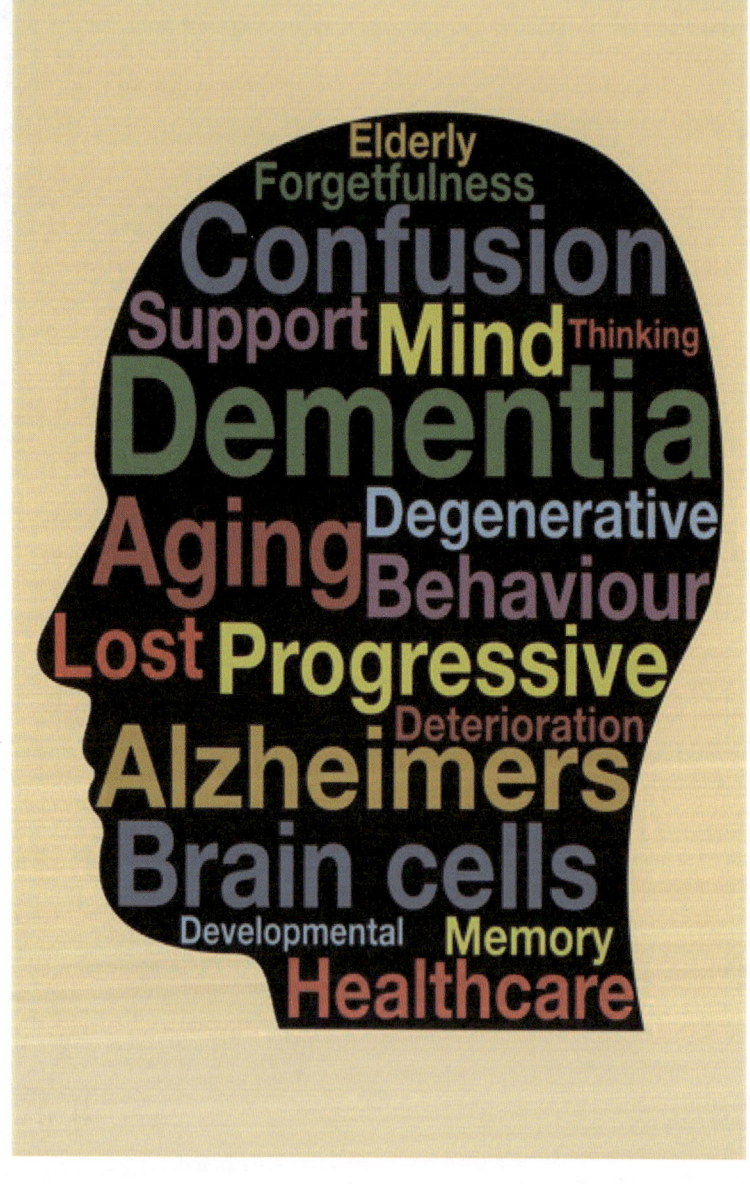

Mental Capacity

The preceding chapters have set out the basic legal landscape of mental health law in Hong Kong. However, it is important to understand the concept of **"Mental Capacity"** before we proceed to the practical considerations in planning the care regime and management of the property and affairs for special needs persons suffering from mental incapacitation.

You may recall that in Case Study 8, Mr F's mental capacity was challenged by his children. After a two-day hearing, the court, having considered the medical reports and heard evidence from the medical experts, the siblings and Mr F himself, decided that Mr F was incapable of handling his property and affairs. I will briefly discuss the concept of **"Capacity"** and the different levels of Capacity required to make decisions with legal effect, such as wills, enduring powers of attorney etc.

When a person has the capacity to make decisions in a reasonable manner, he or she should generally be entitled to make his or her own decisions. Thus, sometimes, a person with symptoms of early stage of dementia may still be considered mentally capable of managing his or her property and affairs or of consenting to or refusing medical treatment, unless he or she is unable to make reasoned decisions.

What Is Capacity?

So, what is the meaning of Capacity? Capacity generally refers to the mental competence of an individual to make a particular decision, and/or undertake certain acts, and/or engage in a particular activity.

> Generally speaking, an individual has the capacity to make a particular decision when he or she can:[1]
>
> 1) understand the facts and the choices involved;
> 2) weigh up the consequences of the decision; and
> 3) communicate the decision.

There is a legal presumption that an individual has Capacity unless the contrary is shown. In other words, **Capacity is presumed**.[2]

Different levels of Capacity are required for different activities, decisions and transactions or dealings.[3] Thus, **Capacity is decision-specific**.

---

1. See "Capacity Toolkit" published by the Attorney General's Department of the New South Wales government.
2. See para 5.01(4) of the Hong Kong Solicitor's Guide to Professional Conduct.
3. See the case of *Re Collis*, unrep. (the UK's Court of Protection, 27 October 2010).

An individual's Capacity can change with time and fluctuate depending on his or her physical or mental condition. That is to say, **Capacity is time-specific**. For example, if a man tripped over and hit his head on the ground today, rendering him unable to make a decision about whether he should give a HK$100,000 gift to his favourite charity, it does not mean that he cannot make the same type of decisions in future.

We should not assume a person lacks Capacity based on his or her age, appearance, disability, behaviour or educational level.

If an individual is judged to lack Capacity to make a decision, any act done or decision taken on that person's behalf must be in that person's best interests.[4]

Importantly, the fact that a person has some form of mental illness requiring a Committee to be appointed to manage his or her financial affairs does not mean he or she will automatically lack mental capacity. If the person has the ability to make simple financial decisions, he or she should be allowed to do so.

For example, if the person knows exactly how much money he or she has to spend on purchasing a mobile phone, the model and colour of the phone as well as what it is needed for, he or she should be allowed to make that decision or similar decisions.

The principles to be applied in assessing a person's Capacity may be summarized as follows:[5]

1) always presume a person has Capacity;
2) Capacity is decision-specific;
3) do not assume a person lacks Capacity based on appearances;
4) assess the person's decision-making ability, not the decision he or she has made;
5) respect a person's privacy; and
6) substitute decision making is a last resort.

Since Capacity is decision specific, I will briefly mention the **different levels of Capacity** when making a will, an enduring power of attorney and the appointment of Committee under Part II of the MHO.

---

4. See BMA Medical Ethics Depart, *Assessment of Mental Capacity: Guidance for Doctors and Lawyers* (The United Kingdom: British Medical Association, 2nd edn, 2008), Chapter 2.5.
5. See the "Capacity Toolkit" published by the Attorney General's Department of the New South Wales government.

Testamentary Capacity

"**Testamentary Capacity**" refers to the ability to make a will. A will is a declaration of a person's wishes in relation to his or her property intended to take effect upon his or her death.[6]

The capacity to make a will is two-fold. Generally, a person making a will (**Testator**) must be at least 18 years old and possess Testamentary Capacity.

In order to make a will, the Testator should be of sound mind, memory and understanding (ie sound disposing mind) and should have sufficient capacity to appreciate the various dispositions of property.[7]

It has been held in a High Court judgment that the mental capacity required to make a will is that the Testator must:

1. understand the nature of the act and its effects;
2. understand the extent of the property of which he is disposing;
3. be able to comprehend and appreciate the claims to which he ought to give effect; and
4. not have disorder of the mind that would poison his affection, pervert his sense of right or prevent the exercise of his natural faculties.

The court will also consider the rationality of a will when considering whether the Testator has Testamentary Capacity.[8] If the will appears to be properly executed and rational, the court will assume that the Testator was of sound disposing mind when he made his will.[9]

If there is any reason to doubt the Testator's mental capacity, it is prudent to engage a medical doctor to assess and certify that the Testator has the relevant capacity when the Testator gives instructions for the will and when the Testator executes the will.[10]

For further reading on solicitors' role in the preparation and execution of wills, refer to Chapter 8: "Will or No Will?".

---

6. Rebecca Ong, *A Guide to Wills and Probate in Hong Kong* (Hong Kong: Sweet & Maxwell, 2014), para 1.002.
7. See *Halsbury's Laws of Hong Kong* (Hong Kong: LexisNexis Hong Kong, 2nd edn, 1995), para 425.036.
8. See *Re Estate of Au Kong Tim (No. 3)* [2017] 4 HKLRD 284, para 47, and *Chiu Man Fu v Chiu Chung Kwan Ying*, unrep., HCAP No 9/2005 (Court of First Instance, 29 June 2016).
9. See *Suttonro v Sadler* (1857) 3 CB (NS) 87 and *Lau Chi Ying v Lau Wai Leung*, unrep., HCAP No 2/2009 (Court of First Instance, 30 December 2011).
10. See *Banks v Goodfellow* (1869–70) LR 5 QB 549.

Enduring Power of Attorney (EPA)

An EPA is a document which allows the person making the EPA (**Donor**) to give directions regarding his property and financial affairs to a trusted third party (**Attorney**).[11] Unlike an ordinary power of attorney, an EPA will not expire upon the Donor becoming mentally incapacitated.[12] An EPA has to be in the form prescribed under section 3 of the Enduring Powers of Attorney Ordinance (Cap 501) (**EPAO**).

The mental capacity required for creating an EPA is defined in section 5 of the EPAO.[13] The Donor must:

> 1) be able to understand the effect of the EPA;
> 2) be able to make a decision to grant an EPA; and
> 3) be able to communicate his or her wish to create an EPA.

This means that the Donor must understand that:[14]

> 1) the Attorney would be able to assume complete authority over his affairs;
> 2) the Attorney would generally be able to do anything with his property which he himself could have done;
> 3) the authority will continue if he should be or become mentally incapable; and
> 4) if the Donor becomes mentally incapable, the power will be irrevocable even without confirmation by the court.

Thus, the Donor, at the time of signing the instrument, must possess the required capacity as mentioned above.[15]

More information regarding the execution, scope and restrictions of an EPA and other planning tools such as the emerging continuing power of attorney (**CPA**) and advance directives (**AD**) can be found in Chapter 7.

Mental Incapacity under Part II MHO Committee Application

If a person is unable to manage and administer his finances, the court has the power to appoint a Committee to manage the finances of the person under

---

11. Section 8 of the EPAO.
12. Section 4 of the EPAO.
13. See further s 2 of the EPAO and s 1A of Powers of Attorney Ordinance (Cap 31).
14. *Re K* [1988] 1 Ch 310, at 316D-E.
15. Section 5(2) of the EPAO.

Part II of the MHO. As mentioned in Chapter 3, a Committee may be necessary in cases where the person did not execute an EPA before he became mentally incapacitated or in certain cases where an EPA had been executed but the Attorney was given insufficient power under the EPA to cover the management of assets of the mentally incapacitated person.

In considering whether to appoint a Committee, the court will consider if a person is, by reason of mental incapacity, unable to manage and administer his property and affairs.

In the application to appoint a Committee, the applicant must include two medical certificates signed by registered medical practitioners stating that the person is incapable of managing and administering his property and affairs, which, as previously mentioned, generally refers to business matters, legal transactions and other dealings of a similar kind.[16]

The court will consider the medical evidence when assessing if the person has the relevant mental capacity.[17] Usually, medical practitioners will use cognitive assessment scores to indicate the person's mental capacity. Please refer to the tests of Mini-Mental State Examination and Montreal Cognitive Assessment below.

The court may also consider the nature and extent of the person's property and affairs[18] and his or her personal information, such as living conditions, family background, family and social responsibilities, the degree of support the person receives, etc.[19]

The time of assessing capacity is the time of the application to the court for appointment of a Committee on behalf of an alleged mentally incapacitated person. Thus, the medical examination and medical certificate in support of the Part II application should be recent, otherwise the court may order for a further updated medical report and/or request the medical experts to attend the relevant hearing.

Common Tools for Assessment of Mental Capacity

The most common tools for assessment of mental capacity include the Montreal Cognitive Assessment (**MoCA**) and the Mini-Mental State Examination (**MMSE**).

The MoCA is a 30-point assessment for cognitive impairment. It assesses short term memory, visuospatial abilities, executive functions, attention, concentration, working memory, language and orientation to time and place.

---

16. Section 7(5) of the MHO.
17. See *CKKK v CKB*, unrep., CACV No 162/2015 (Court of Appeal, 30 September 2016), paras 23–31.
18. *Martin Masterman-Lister v Jewel & Home Counties Dairies* [2002] EWHC 417 (QB), para 21.
19. Ibid., para 25.

The MMSE is another 30-point assessment to determine cognitive impairment. The assessment categories include orientation to time, orientation to place, registration, attention and calculation, recall, language, repetition and complex commands.

What to Expect at a Mental Assessment

At the mental assessment, a person would be expected to attend a consultation with the doctor which may last between 15 minutes to one hour, depending on the circumstances.

The consultation is mainly oral in nature and would normally involve the doctor asking the subject simple questions relating to his or her daily affairs and testing his or her short term memory.

Common Causes of Mental Incapacity

The common causes of mental incapacity are:

> 1) a congenital intellectual disability;
> 2) acquired brain damage due to injury or illness;
> 3) substance abuse; or
> 4) dementia, Alzheimer's disease, autism, bipolar disorder, cerebral vascular disease, cognitive disorder, dementia, epilepsy, hallucination/delusions, post-traumatic stress disorder, psychopathic disorder, schizophrenia, stroke and vascular neurocognitive disorder or other psychiatric condition.[20]

What Is Dementia?

Since dementia is one of the most common causes of mental incapacity in our ageing population, it may be helpful to discuss in layman's terms what dementia is, especially when not all persons with dementia are incapable of managing and administering their property and affairs.

Dementia is often described as a syndrome in which there is deterioration of brain functions including memory, thinking, behaviour and ability to perform everyday activities. Although dementia mainly affects older people, it is not a normal part of ageing.[21] It is caused by a variety of diseases and

---

20. See Appendix I.
21. See the World Health Organization's Fact Sheet on Dementia dated 12 December 2017, available at http://www.who.int/news-room/fact-sheets/detail/dementia.

injuries that affect the brain, such as stroke or Alzheimer's disease, which is an irreversible degenerative disorder of the brain that destroys brain cells and nerves disrupting the transmitters which carry messages in the brain, particularly those responsible for storing memory.

Dementia is usually progressive in nature and starts with deterioration in mental or brain functions mentioned above leading to total dependence on others and requiring different levels of services. The signs and symptoms linked to dementia can be broadly classified into three stages:

1. Early stage

Common symptoms of the early stage of dementia include:
a) forgetfulness;
b) losing track of time; and
c) becoming lost in familiar places.

2. Middle stage

Common symptoms of the middle stage of dementia include:
a) becoming forgetful of recent events and people's names;
b) becoming lost at home;
c) having increasing difficulty with communication;
d) needing help with personal care; and
e) experiencing behavioural changes, including wandering and repeated questioning.

3. Late stage

Common symptoms of the late stage of dementia include:
a) becoming unaware of the time and place;
b) having difficulty in recognizing relatives and friends;
c) having an increasing need for assisted self-care;
d) having difficulty in walking; and
e) experiencing behavioural changes that may escalate and include aggression.

According to a study conducted by researchers from the University of Hong Kong and the Chinese University of Hong Kong,[22] the number of people aged 60 or above with dementia is projected to increase by 222%, from 103,433 in 2009 to 332,688 in 2039, with a large proportion of those persons living in institutions.

The prevalence rates of dementia in Hong Kong are estimated to be 8% among persons aged over 65 and 20% to 30% among those aged over 80 years old.[23] In other words, about 1 in every 10 persons aged between 65 to 79 years old and 1 in every 3 persons aged 80 years old or above will likely be suffering from dementia.

Since there does not appear to be any effective treatment to cure dementia, it is important to provide as much support as we can to improve the lives of people with dementia and their carers and families,[24] such as:

1) early diagnosis in order to promote early and optimal management;
2) optimizing physical health, cognition, activity and well-being;
3) identifying and treating accompanying physical illness;
4) detecting and treating challenging behavioural and psychological symptoms; and
5) providing information and long-term support to carers.

Dementia is a progressive neurological disorder and, thus far, no cure or effective treatment has been found. Experts have devised many cognitive activities and programs to help to improve the lives of people with dementia, delay deterioration and build up cognitive reserve so as to reduce the impact of dementia in the community.

According to recommendations from the Hong Kong Alzheimer's Disease Association, there are ways to reduce our chances of developing dementia and maintain a healthy lifestyle to promote good mental health.

It has been found that social interaction, cultivating music and arts appreciation, regular physical exercise, reading, and learning to use computers

---

22. Ruby Yu et al., "Trends in Prevalence and Mortality of Dementia in Elderly Hong Kong Population: Projections, Disease Burden, and Implications for Long Term Care" (2012) *International Journal of Alzheimer's Disease*.
23. See the article "Care services for elderly persons with dementia" on the website of the Hong Kong Legislative Council, available at https://www.legco.gov.hk/research-publications/english/essentials-1617ise10-care-services-for-elderly-persons-with-dementia.htm#endnote2.
24. See the World Health Organization's Fact Sheet on Dementia dated 12 December 2017, available at http://www.who.int/news-room/fact-sheets/detail/dementia.

and other information technology to stimulate the executive functioning of the brain will delay deterioration and build up cognitive reserve.

For more information on this topic, visit the website of World Health Organization, available at http://www.who.int/mediacentre/factsheets/fs362/en/

and the website of Hong Kong Alzheimer's Disease Association, available at http://www.hkada.org.hk/en/?page_id=1840.

Part II

5
Ways to Protect and Manage the Mentally Incapacitated Person's (MIP) Property and Affairs

Many parents of adult children with special needs arising from conditions like severe autism or Down syndrome are concerned with how to plan for the financial needs of their children when they themselves grow old. Similarly, carers for elderly family members suffering from dementia and other forms of mental incapacity are increasingly concerned about how to protect their elderly family members from financial abuse.

As explained in Chapter 3, a guardian may be appointed under Part IVB of the MHO for any person aged 18 years or above with decision-making incapacity regarding his welfare and personal circumstances. However, there is a monthly financial limit (currently set at HK$17,000)[1] in the powers given to the guardian for the maintenance or benefit of the person under guardianship.

Thus, if an adult with decision-making incapacity owns landed properties or cash and stocks, a Committee under Part II of the MHO may need to be appointed, especially where there are disputes between family members, suspicious or actual improper dealings with that person's assets, a person has signed an agreement to buy or sell a property but becomes an MIP before completion, and so on.

The focus in this chapter is on the issues commonly faced by family members and carers of an MIP and the circumstances in which they should seek legal advice or assistance on how to protect and manage the property and affairs of mentally incapacitated persons, with reference to some of the modified case studies in Chapter 1. Broadly speaking, there are three categories of special needs persons that may need protection:

1) adult children with special needs;
2) elderly persons with deteriorating cognitive function and behavioural changes; and
3) persons with acquired brain injury due to accidents.

---

1. Section 59R(3)(f) and s 44B(8) of the MHO.

Adult Children with Special Needs

In Case Study 1, Mr and Mrs A's only son, X, was diagnosed with severe autism and global development delay since his childhood. Although X was 25 years old, his mental age was only 10 years old. X had recently inherited a residential property in Hong Kong from his paternal grandfather who had passed away.

You may recall that Mrs A made a Part II application in the Mental Health Court to be appointed as the Committee of X to manage the property and financial affairs of X, including renting out the property and depositing the rental income into a newly opened Committee's account solely for X's use and benefit which included payment of X's medical and other therapy fees.

Mr and Mrs A cared for X since he was born. While X was a child under 18 years of age, Mr and Mrs A had all parental rights and responsibilities towards X. However, when X turned 18 years old, although legally speaking he was an adult, his mental age was that of a child. Therefore, Mr and Mrs A continued to look after X as if he was a child, attending to his daily care, medical treatment and financial affairs.

The situation became more complicated when X inherited his late grandfather's property. X had no mental capacity to sign legal documents and his parents began to worry about who would look after X's welfare, property and financial affairs when they grew old or became incapacitated. They were also worried about the possibility that X might sign away his assets to third parties against his best interests.

Mr and Mrs A considered setting up a trust with a reputable bank in Hong Kong, appointing trustees and a case manager to devise a care plan for the benefit of X, and setting out in a letter of wishes to the trustees how they wished to use the trust funds to pay for the expenditure of X as their dependent beneficiary under the trust.

However, due to insufficient knowledge and experience as to the operation of a trust, and considering the recurring administrative costs of the proposed trust to be quite substantial, Mr and Mrs A did not feel comfortable to set up a trust and transfer their assets into the trust for the benefit of X during their lifetime.

When Mr and Mrs A met with solicitors who were experienced in this area of law, they considered the best option at the time to be to take out a Part II application and appoint Mrs A as the Committee of X to handle his property and affairs. Mrs A understood that, as the Committee of X, she would have to keep proper monthly income and expenditure accounts and submit an annual account of how she had dealt with the money and assets she received and spent on X's behalf. Mrs A was happy and willing to do so, since she believed that this would set a good blueprint for whoever was appointed as Committee to look after X when Mrs and Mr A grew old or became incapacitated, or for whatever other reason were no longer able to manage the property and affairs of X.

Thus the issues faced by Mr and Mrs A included:

> 1) X's mental capacity to sign legal documents;
> 2) whether it was necessary and appropriate to appoint a Committee to manage the property and affairs of X even though there was no dispute between family members nor suspicious improper dealings of X's assets;
> 3) whether it was necessary and appropriate to set up a trust for the benefit of X;
> 4) who was the most appropriate person to be appointed as trustee or Committee of X; and
> 5) the duties and responsibilities of the Committee, etc.

The issues faced by Mr and Mrs A are not uncommon. If you wish to learn more about the scope and powers of a Committee, refer to Chapter 3, Practice Direction 30.1 and the "Guidance Notes to Persons appointed as Committee of Estate of an MIP".[2]

Special Needs Trusts

It is understandable that many parents are worried about the care of their children with special needs after they pass away, especially for those who are unable to afford the cost of setting up a private trust.

In response to concerns and demands from parents and the general public, the Hong Kong government in its Policy Address 2017 decided to take the lead in setting up a "Special Needs Trust" (**SNT**).

In gist, the proposal is for the Director of Social Welfare (**DSW**) to act as the trustee to provide reliable and affordable trust services, so that the trustee will manage the assets of deceased parents and make regular disbursements to the carers of their children (who may be individuals or organizations). The trustee will follow the parents' wishes for the long-term daily needs of their children.

The SNT is intended to be launched by the end of 2018.[3] The proposed framework is as follows.

---

2. This is available at www.judiciary.hk/en/crt_services/pphlt/html/guidance_note.htm#1.
3. See the presentation slides for the "Briefing on the Proposed Framework on Special Needs Trust" organized by the Hong Kong government on 12 February 2018.

Legal framework

1. The DSW shall be a corporation sole and shall have the name of the Director of Social Welfare Incorporated (**DSWI**) under the Director of Social Welfare Incorporation Ordinance (Cap 1096) and in that name shall have perpetual succession.
2. The DSWI may act as trustee of any trust created for the benefit of persons in the care of the Social Welfare Department or of any trust created in connection with the work of the said Department.
3. The DSWI shall invest any trust funds and assets in any investment according to the Trustee Ordinance (Cap 29) and shall discharge the statutory duty of care.

Relevant documents

1. The parents (**Settlors**) will need to sign a trust deed together with a letter of intent and care plan with the DSWI to set up the trust.
2. The parents will also need to execute a will to inject funds into the said trust upon their demise.
3. The DSWI will provide a template of the trust deed and the suggested clauses to be included in the Settlors' wills.
4. The Settlors should carefully formulate the specifics clearly in the letter of intent and care plan for the need of the beneficiary children with special needs.
5. The DSWI as trustee will pool together the funds from different trust accounts for investment in a single investment portfolio to reduce administration and other costs.

Financial management

1. Profits or losses from the investment will be allocated to the different trust accounts on pro-rata basis.
2. Regular disbursements will be made according to the specific care plan to the carer of the beneficiary children with special needs.
3. Only cash will be accepted by the DSWI as trustee and the DSWI will hold the cash on trust under the SNT arrangement.
4. Periodic payment or contributions by the Settlors or annuity from the estate will not be accepted to minimize administrative costs.[4]

---

4. However, some parents have in the consultation briefings requested the government to consider accepting one off contributions by relatives of the settlors or other persons concerned with the welfare of the beneficiaries with special needs. The government indicated

5. The trust account will be terminated a) when the beneficiary passes away and the remaining cash funds will be handled in accordance with the trust deed; or b) when the funds have been exhausted, in which case, the beneficiary may be referred to the relevant social welfare service.

Operational procedure

1. The Settlor sets up a trust account together with a trust deed, letter of intent and care plan and executes a will when alive as mentioned above.
2. When the Settlor passes away, the executor appointed by the Settlor in the will is to realize the Settlor's assets and transfer the funds into the trust account so as to activate the trust account.
3. The DSWI as trustee will pool together funds from different parents' trust accounts to make investments and deposit the profits (if any) to the respective accounts, manage the accounts and pay regular disbursements to the carer designated by the Settlor in accordance with the trust deed.
4. The carer will execute the care plan designated for the beneficiary children with special needs.
5. The DSWI as trustee will review the execution of the care plan regularly until termination.

Considerations

In preparing the letter of intent and care plan, the Settlor should consider the expected lifestyle of his children in future, the related expenses and funds to be reserved and a sustainable care plan. Since the care plan is for the benefit of the beneficiary children with special needs, the Settlor should involve them and respect their views as much as possible in formulating the care plan.

The efforts of the government, in particular the Commissioner of Rehabilitation, the Director of Social Welfare and Professors Ho and Lee of the University of Hong Kong Faculty of Law in the setting up of the SNT deserve praise and recognition. However, Hong Kong still has a long way to go in the protection of children with special needs and the provision of

---

that they may consider what would be the most cost-effective way to accept contributions to the trust when the funds are about to be depleted.

support and peace of mind to parents who have concerns as to who will look after their children when they grow old or pass away.

Elderly Persons with Deteriorating Cognitive Function and Behavioural Changes

In Case Study 2, Mr Y, who was in his mid-80s, was hit by a car while crossing the road on his way to work one morning. As a result of the injuries he suffered severe brain damage and required 24-hour nursing care, regular physiotherapy, occupational therapy and speech therapy.

You may recall that Mr Y had three sons working in the family business founded by Mr Y, and while Mr Y was hospitalized they had discovered some irregular lump sum withdrawals from Mr Y's personal bank account.

After seeking legal advice from solicitors and making necessary enquiries with Mr Y's accountant, the three sons did not make a report to the police regarding the lump sum withdrawals. They discovered that Mr Y had given written authorization to his female business partner with whom he had a close relationship, ie Ms C, who had made those lump sum withdrawals.

Mr Y's sons eventually decided to apply collectively to be appointed as the Committee of Mr Y under Part II of the MHO to protect their elderly father from any potential financial abuse and to properly manage the property and affairs of their father.

Although it transpired that there may not have been any financial abuse or unauthorized withdrawals from Mr Y's account, Mr Y's sons considered that it was still necessary to have a Committee appointed to look after Mr Y's business and financial affairs.

Furthermore, since the driver of the car that ran into Mr Y was subsequently convicted of the offence of reckless driving, the Committee also took out legal proceedings against the said driver as Mr Y's next friend and claimed damages as a result of the driver's negligence.[5]

Thus the issues faced by Mr Y's sons included:

1. whether it was necessary to report to the police for suspicious improper dealings with Mr Y's assets and/or suspected financial abuse;
2. whether a Committee should be appointed to properly manage the property and affairs of Mr Y, in particular his business and financial assets;

---

5. See Ord 80 of the Rules of the High Court (Cap 4) which governs the participation in legal proceedings of people under a disability.

3. whether the Committee had power to make provision for maintenance of or benefiting Mr Y's family members;
4. whether the Committee had power to make provisions for other persons, such as Ms C who Mr Y had been supporting financially prior to becoming an MIP;
5. who had the right to issue proceedings to claim damages against the driver of the car who ran into Mr Y negligently, after the driver was convicted of reckless driving;
6. who was the most appropriate person to be appointed as Committee of Mr Y; and
7. the duties and responsibilities of the Committee, etc.

Thus, in addition to taking out a Part II application under the MHO to set up a care regime and pay for the daily expenditure of Mr Y, the sons also had to seek legal advice on how to deal with Ms C's potential claim for making financial provisions for her and on commencing legal proceedings against the driver of the car who ran into Mr Y.

Persons with Acquired Brain Injury Due to Accidents

You have read in Case Study 2 how Mr Y suffered from severe brain damage as a result of a traffic accident and all the issues faced by his family members. Similarly, in Case Study 11, Mr and Mrs B also faced a range of issues when their 8-year-old daughter, AB, was hit by a truck while she was walking back home from school and tragically suffered severe brain damage necessitating numerous operations.

AB suffers from dystonic quadriplegic cerebral palsy and doctors have advised that she will be dependent on gastronomy feeding and specialist care for the rest of her life. Since Mr and Mrs B have limited financial resources, they applied for legal aid to issue legal proceedings against the truck driver and a rather large settlement was reached and paid into the court.

Similarly, in Case Study 12, Mr Q was a construction worker who suffered severe injuries in an industrial accident rendering him a paraplegic. Since Mr Q was the sole breadwinner of the family, Mrs Q also applied for legal aid to take out legal proceedings against the employer/tortfeasor and a substantial settlement sum was awarded to Mr Q. In this case, Mrs Q unfortunately suffered from severe depression and personality disorder and was unable to look after Mr Q's property and affairs.

The common issues faced by Mr and Mrs B as well as Mrs Q included:

1. how to issue legal proceedings against the driver or employer/tortfeasor for personal injuries/negligence on behalf of a mentally disabled person;
2. how to map out a comprehensive care regime and apply for money to be released from the court for victims of traffic accidents and industrial accidents;
3. how to invest the settlement sum for the benefit and care of the severely injured victims; and
4. how to prepare the necessary accounts and reports to the court as the Committee's reports.

You should seek legal advice if you encounter these issues. If you think you may be eligible for legal aid, please visit the website of the Legal Aid Department and make enquiries.[6]

How to Invest Damages Awarded to an MIP in a Personal Injury Claim

In most personal injuries claims, damages awarded to MIPs are paid into the court for the MIP to earn interest at the Suitors' Fund rate until there is an application for payment out by the Committee appointed for the MIP. These damages can be quite substantial in serious personal injury cases. The majority of these funds are placed in fixed deposits with commercial banks ranging from one to six months in duration. The net rate of return is set out on page 71.

---

6. See www.lad.gov.hk.

Period	Average annual interest rates (%)	Inflation/deflation according to Composite Consumer Price Index based on June values (being halfway through the year) (%)	Net rate of return (%)
1 January to 31 December 2007	4.30	1.3	3
1 January to 31 December 2008	2.48	6.1	−3.62
1 January to 31 December 2009	0.52	−0.9	1.42
1 January to 31 December 2010	0.33	2.8	−2.47
1 January to 31 December 2011	0.69	5.6	−4.91
1 January to 31 December 2012	0.91	3.7	−2.79
1 January to 31 December 2013	0.71	4.1	−3.39
1 January to 31 December 2014	0.74	3.6	−2.86
1 January to 31 December 2015	0.60	3.1	−2.5
1 January to 31 December 2016	0.67	2.4	−1.73
1 January to 1 September 2017	0.61	1.9	−1.29

The discount rate is a reflection of the interest rate or rate of return from investment. Thus, the higher the discount rate, the lower the multiplier, resulting in a lower final award to be made to the injured person.

In the case of *Chan Pak Ting v Chan Chi Kuen (No. 2)* [2013] 2 HKLRD 1, Mr Justice Mohan Bharwaney concluded in his judgment that the previous net rate of return of 4.5% per annum was no longer valid in Hong Kong due to significant changes in the economic landscape since the judgment of *Chan Pui Ki v Leung On* in 1996. He set out a discount rate for plaintiffs with future needs in excess of 10 years at 2.5% net of inflation.

However, the net rate of return, ie net of inflation of 2.5% per annum, cannot be achieved if funds are kept in court earning interest at the Suitors' Fund rate.[7] In his judgment, Mr Justice Mohan Bharwaney offered some guidance on the type of investment portfolio that may suitably compensate claimants with needs exceeding 10 years, which can be roughly summarized as follows (see page 72):

---

7. See paras 68 and 96 of the judgment in *Chan Pak Ting*.

1. 10% in time deposits;
2. 70% in high quality bonds of a rating of BBB+ or better; and
3. 20% in high quality blue chip stock that qualifies as "widows and orphans" stock.

Thus, Committees appointed on behalf of the claimants who are under disability should seek proper legal advice on how to make an application to the Mental Health Court on behalf of the MIP to invest a substantial part of the damages received.

Since Hong Kong does not have a Court of Protection, the Judiciary may consider whether or not it would be more cost effective and beneficial to the claimants under disability for the Personal Injury Judge to take over as the Mental Health Judge after the settlement, since he or she may be in a better position to understand the care regime that needs to be set up for the claimant.

6
Practical Considerations on How to Manage Assets of the MIP

Chapter 3 sets out the procedures for the appointment of a Committee under Part II of the MHO. In this chapter, we will look at how the assets of the MIP should be managed after the Committee has been appointed.

A good place to start is the "Guidance Note to Persons appointed as Committee of Estate of a Mentally Incapacitated Person" (**Guidance Note**) published by the Judiciary,[1] a copy of which is given to the newly appointed Committee by the court after an Appointment Order has been made.

The Guidance Note sets out the powers and duties of a Committee and certain steps that the Committee should take. The Guidance Note also contains a specimen of the statement of accounts that has to be submitted to the court, usually on an annual basis, as specified in the court order. The Guidance Note is appended at the end of this chapter.

When acting as a Committee, it is always important to check the relevant court order(s) or directions as to the powers and authorities given and specific duties to be performed. These may vary from case to case. A copy of the standard order which is annexed to PD 30.1 can be found at the end of this chapter.

Different Types of MIPs' Assets

An MIP may have a wide-ranging list of assets covering cash, stocks, valuables in safe deposit boxes, landed properties and personal chattels. We will look at how these different types of assets should be managed by a Committee below.

I. Cash

Cash is the most common form of assets of an MIP, sometimes the only major form.

---

1. See www.judiciary.hk/en/crt_services/pphlt/html/guidance_note.htm.

The order appointing a Committee will always provide for the power of the Committee to open bank accounts. This is important as the Committee should always keep separate accounts for the MIP's assets. Since it takes some time to open a separate Committee's bank account, this is usually one of the first things a Committee will do when appointed.

The Committee should note that not all banks in Hong Kong are familiar with the opening of a Committee's bank account and it is always best for the Committee to enquire with a number of banks to find out their bank account opening policies, quality of service and the interest rates for comparison.

Once a Committee's bank account has been opened, the Committee should write to the different banks at which the MIP used to keep his or her accounts (including savings, current and fixed deposit accounts) for the transfer of funds in the MIP's account to the Committee's bank account. Thereafter, the bank accounts in the name of the MIP can be closed.

Sometimes, it may also be necessary for the Committee to write to different banks to ascertain if the MIP has an account with the particular bank and, if so, to require the bank to close the MIP's account and transfer the funds to the Committee's account.

It is not uncommon for elderly MIPs in Hong Kong to keep cash at home, stashed in cookie jars or mooncake tins underneath their beds. If a Committee comes across cash at home, it has a duty to keep proper account and deposit the same into the Committee's bank accounts.

II. Stocks

Stocks and shares in companies can be in the form of physical scripts or in securities accounts with banks or brokers. Physical scripts have to be properly stored (eg in the Committee's safe deposit box) and shares in a securities account can be transferred into the Committee's securities account.

Share registrars have to be notified of the appointment of the Committee. If there is no immediate need to realize the shares for the MIP's maintenance, the shares are generally kept according to the MIP's original investment preference.

However, if the Committee wishes to engage stock brokers and bankers to advise on the MIP's assets and investment management of the MIP's stocks, the Committee should obtain all relevant information including the fees and company portfolio of the brokers and details of the investment product and its net investment returns, and set out reasons for making such investment decision in the Committee report on investment.[2]

---

2. See para 8 of the Annex F to PD30.1.

III. Safe deposit box

If the MIP has safe deposit boxes with banks, the Committee will need to take inventory of these and transfer the contents into a safe deposit box opened by the Committee pursuant to the court order.

Arrangements will have to be made with various banks to check the availability of empty safe deposit boxes and it is recommended that security guards be engaged for the transfer of contents between different banks should it be necessary.

IV. Landed property

The Committee should register the court order with the Land Registry, take possession of the landed properties held in the name of the MIP and change the locks where appropriate. Since there may be various concerns and complexities involved in the registration of the order, please seek proper legal advice in this regard.

In order to preserve the assets of the MIP, the Committee should arrange for insurance to be taken out to cover the landed properties and to maintain proper repair.

Expenses relating to the landed properties such as management fees and government rates and rent should be paid out of the MIP's assets by the Committee and the Rating and Valuation Department should be notified of the change of contact.

Where the landed properties are investment properties, the Committee should, having checked that it has the express power and authority to do so in the court order, renew or sign new tenancy agreements on behalf of the MIP in order to generate rental income.

If no express power is provided, the Committee should consider seeking the court's direction for the renting out of the properties. If the properties require major renovation or repair works (eg building orders), specific approval and directions will be required.

The powers of management of the estate do not extend to the sale or charge by way of mortgage or letting of immovable landed property unless for a term of not exceeding three years.[3]

If in doubt, the Committee should seek legal assistance and clarification from the court, as most important decisions in relation to the landed properties of the MIP must be approved by the court.

---

3. Section 12 of the MHO.

V. Personal chattels

Depending on the nature of the personal chattels, they may need special storage facilities and caretaking (eg in the case of paintings and antiques). Valuables will also require proper insurance coverage.

VI. Social welfare

If the MIP has been receiving social security or old age or disability allowance, the Committee should contact the relevant District Officer of the Social Welfare Department to arrange for future allowances to be paid into the Committee's bank account.

VII. Transfer of Hong Kong property when the MIP resides overseas

If the MIP is residing outside Hong Kong, the court may, upon being satisfied that the person has been declared to be mentally incapacitated and that his personal estate has been vested in a Committee, curator or manager according to the laws of the place where he or she is residing, order the transfer of property situated in Hong Kong to such Committee, curator or manager as the court may think fit.[4]

Payments to Be Made on Behalf of an MIP

While the Committee is not responsible for making decisions as to the accommodation and medical treatment of the MIP, the Committee is responsible for paying for such expenses. If the MIP is staying at an elderly home or hospital, the Committee should make arrangements with the home or hospital for the payment of expenses incurred by the MIP.

Thus, examples of payments to be made on behalf of the MIP include:

>   1) accommodation expenses including utilities;
>   2) food and household expenses;
>   3) domestic helpers and other professional carers;
>   4) transport;
>   5) personal grooming and attire;
>   6) medical treatment;
>   7) holidays;

---

4. Section 23 of the MHO.

8) tax and insurance;
9) dependent family members etc.

Practical Considerations When Appointed as the Committee

Here are some practical steps for you to consider when you are appointed as the Committee. You should consult your lawyer or seek further directions or clarification from the court if you have any queries.

1. Court Order or Committee Order

The court order appointing you as the Committee contains all the powers of the Committee in dealing with the MIP's property and affairs (commonly referred to as "**Committee Order**"). Please check the powers of the Committee Order carefully. If you wish to take any steps that are not covered in the Committee Order, please apply to the court for specific directions or consult a lawyer specializing in this area of law.

Please ensure that sufficient sealed copies of the Committee Order are obtained for use.

2. Opening Committee's bank accounts

Once you have been appointed as the Committee, make arrangements with a licensed bank to open a Committee's bank account. It usually takes at least four to six weeks for an account to be opened, thus this step should be taken as soon as possible.

Usually three accounts are opened: a current account, a savings account and a securities account, depending on the size and nature of the liquid assets of the MIP.

Most banks in Hong Kong require a sealed copy of the Committee Order to be produced for account opening purposes.

3. Notifying relevant parties or organizations of your appointment

Once the Committee Order has been sealed, write to the following organizations. Please note that this list is for guidance only and is not exhaustive:

1) banks which the MIP has kept accounts with to arrange for the transfer of the MIP's monies into the Committee's bank account (if any);
2) companies or brokers for handing over of shares (if any);
3) the Social Welfare Department in respect of disability or old age allowances (if any);
4) any persons or institutions holding monies or assets on behalf of the MIP;
5) government bodies such as the Inland Revenue Department or Rating and Valuation Department if the MIP pays income tax and/or holds landed properties; and
6) management and utilities companies if the MIP holds landed properties.

4. Safe deposit box

If the MIP holds a safe deposit box at his or her bank, make arrangements to open the safe deposit box, make an inventory of contents and transfer the contents to another safe deposit box opened in the name of the Committee where appropriate and necessary.

5. Landed property

If the MIP holds landed properties, the Committee will need to make arrangements for the preservation of the properties, including but not limited to the following:

1) obtaining title deeds to the property;
2) inspecting the property and changing locks as appropriate;
3) registering the sealed Committee Order at the Land Registry;
4) taking out property and contents insurance as appropriate and necessary;
5) notifying the management office and arranging settlement of management fees, etc;
6) notifying the Rating & Valuation Department for payment of rates; and
7) notifying the tenants and arranging payment of rental fees into the Committee's bank account as appropriate.

6. Will or power of attorney

The Committee should make enquiries on the existence of the MIP's will and power of attorney and, if found, keep these documents in safe custody.

The Committee should also consider whether a statutory will is necessary and, if so, inform the court accordingly. For more information on a statutory will, refer to Chapter 8: "Will or No Will?".

7. Monthly payments

The Committee should obtain original invoices for sums which need to be paid for the benefit of the MIP. In cases where payments are not receipted, the Committee should obtain written confirmation from the payee as to what the amount was spent on and monitor the expenses regularly.

8. Keeping accounts

The Committee should pay all the money received on the MIP's behalf into the Committee's bank account and make all payments on the MIP's behalf from the Committee's bank account. It is important for the Committee to keep all bank statements, receipts and invoices.

9. Change in the MIP's situation

The Committee must inform the court if:

> 1) the MIP has any further assets or if he or she inherits any properties or money;
> 2) the MIP is likely to get married, divorced or be involved in any legal proceedings;
> 3) the MIP recovers and no longer requires the Committee to assist in managing and administrating his properties and affairs; or
> 4) the MIP passes away.

10. Acting in the best interests of the MIP

The Committee must act in the best interests of the MIP at all times and ensure that the MIP's money is being used to provide the MIP with the best quality of life.

Thus, if the Committee does not know the MIP personally, it is useful to get to know the MIP and make appropriate enquires with close friends and relatives to learn more about the MIP's likes and dislikes, wishes, beliefs and past decision making when he or she once had mental capacity.

Figure 6.1: Steps to Take upon Appointment as Committee

1. Get to know the MIP and his/her needs
2. Check your Court Order for powers
3. Ascertain and verify MIP's assets and open Committee bank accounts
4. Notify relevant parties of your appointment
5. Take possession of and preserve MIP's property and assets
6. Arrange monthly payments for benefit of MIP
7. Keep proper accounts with supporting receipts and invoices
8. Submit annual report to the Court

Guidance Note to Persons appointed as Committee of Estate of a Mentally Incapacitated Person ("MIP")

Pursuant to Part II of the Mental Health Ordinance, Cap. 136, you have been appointed as committee of the estate of a MIP to manage and administer his/her property and affairs. The purpose of this Note is to give you information about your role and responsibility as a committee. This Note also highlights certain steps you need to take as committee. In case of doubt, you should consult your lawyer or seek further directions or clarification from the Court.

Power of a committee

The court order appointing you will clearly set out your powers. You will note that such powers are limited to dealing with the MIP's property and financial affairs.

Your powers come to an end when:
a) the Court is satisfied that the MIP has recovered; or
b) the MIP dies; or
c) another committee is appointed to replace you.

Duties of a committee

You have a duty to:
- act in the best interest of the MIP at all times
- make sure that the MIP's money is being used to give him/her the best quality of life
- comply with all Court directions and Orders
- open a committee bank account
- look after the MIP's property
- make sure all income is collected and all bills are paid on time
- claim all social security benefits that are due to the MIP
- prepare accounts every year or whenever the Court needs you to
- keep all important documents and other valuable items in a safe place
- keep the MIP's landed property secure, in a reasonable state of repair, and adequately insured
- deal with the MIP's tax matters
- obtain Court's prior approval before dealing with the MIP's savings and/or investments

- inform the Court about any changes in the MIP's financial situation, e.g. if you discover any further assets of the MIP or if he/she inherits any property or money
- inform the Court if there is a likelihood of the MIP getting married, divorced or involved in any legal proceedings
- inform the Court if preparation of a statutory will is being considered
- inform the Court about any changes in the MIP's address and accommodation fees
- inform the Court of the MIP's recovery
- inform the Court if the MIP dies

Obtaining Court's directions

You should note that once a person has been found by the Court to be a MIP, all dealings with regard to his/her estate, including assets and finance, have to be approved by the Court.

Although you are the committee of the estate of the MIP, it does not mean that you can deal with the MIP's property and financial affairs as you wish. You must check the Order appointing you to ensure that you have the power to do a particular act on behalf of the MIP. In other words if you wish to sell the MIP's landed property, stocks and shares, you need a specific direction in the Court Order to enable you to do so.

When you need to do something on behalf of the MIP which you have not been empowered to do by the Order appointing you, you must apply to the Court, for specific authority to do so. Such application should be made to the Registrar, High Court by letter together with supporting documents unless otherwise directed by the Court. In case of doubt, you should consult your lawyer.

Some steps which, as committee, you need to take:

1. The committee bank account

When you are appointed committee, you should open a committee bank account. You will need to show the bank the Court Order appointing you as committee. Once the committee bank account is open, you must deposit into the account all monies belonging to the MIP. You must arrange for any benefits or income of the MIP to be paid into the committee bank account.

You must always keep the MIP's money separate from your own money.

2. Notice

You should give notice to all relevant authorities (such as Inland Revenue, Land Registry, electricity, gas and water suppliers) that you are now acting as the MIP's committee.

3. Keeping accounts

One of the things you will have to do is to provide an account each year (or for whatever period of the Court has specified) of how you have dealt with the money you received and spent on the MIP's behalf. The duty to provide accounts is usually specified in the Court Order appointing you.

You will find it easier to prepare the accounts if you:
a) pay all money you receive on MIP's behalf into the committee bank account;
b) make all payments on the MIP's behalf from the account; and
c) keep all bank statements, receipts and invoices

A specimen statement of accounts is attached to this Guidance Note for your reference.

If you fail to provide accounts as ordered, you risk being discharged as the MIP's committee and you may also be sued by the MIP.

MONTHLY ACCOUNT of the estate of [Name of Mentally Incapacitated Person] _____ **Month/Year:** ____/____ *(completed monthly)*

Income			Expenditure		Receipts	
Items	Amount		Items	Amount	Yes	No
1. Social Security Allowance	$		1. Nursing Home Fee/Rental	$		
2. Pension	$		2. Diaper Fees	$		
3. Interest/Dividend *(e.g. Bank accounts/Shares)*			3. Medical expenses *(e.g. medical consultation, hospitalization fees, physiotherapist charges, etc)*			
(1)	$		(1)	$		
(2)	$		(2)	$		
(3)	$		(3)	$		
4. Rental Income *(list address of the properties)*			4. Domestic helper	$		
(1)	$		5. Private nurse	$		
(2)	$		6. Food	$		
			7. Transport	$		
			8. Utilities (e.g. electricity, gas, rates, telephone, water)	$		
5. Proceeds from selling of shares/properties			9. Other expenses *(please specify)*			
(1)	$		(1)	$		
(2)	$		(2)	$		
6. Contributions from family members	$		10. Repayment of Debts			
7. Others *(please specify)*			(1)	$		
(1)	$		(2)	$		
(2)	$					
Total:	**$**		**Total:**	**$**		

Signed by the Committee: _____

Date: _____

(*Please keep all the invoices or receipts and provide copies to the Court)

YEARLY REPORT of the estate of [Name of Mentally Incapacitated Person] as at: [*dd/mm/yy*]
(completed yearly)

Month	Income	Expenditure	Balance
Amount brought forward			$
January	$	$	$
February	$	$	$
March	$	$	$
April	$	$	$
May	$	$	$
June	$	$	$
July	$	$	$
August	$	$	$
September	$	$	$
October	$	$	$
November	$	$	$
December	$	$	$
		Total: Surplus/Deficit	$

Signed by the Committee:_____

Date:_____

(*Separate breakdown for each month to be provided in the form of Monthly Account)

ASSETS of the estate of [Name of Mentally Incapacitated Person] as at: [dd/mm/yy]
(completed yearly)

Assets	Value as at *dd.mm.yy*	*If any of the Assets were sold within this period, please specify*			
		Date of Selling	Selling Price	Deduction of Costs (if any)	Net Value
1. Bank Accounts *(please state name of bank & account no.)*					
(1)	$				
(2)	$				
2. Shares/Equity/Bonds/Funds					
(1)	$				
(2)	$				
(3)	$				
(4)	$				
3. Landed Properties					
(1)	$				
(2)	$				
(3)	$				
4. Items in Safe Deposit Boxes					
(1)					
(2)					
5. Other Assets e.g. life policies, jewellery, cars, antiques, etc					
(1)	$				
(2)	$				

Signed by the Committee:______________________

Date:______________________

(*Please provide the Court with copies of bank statements, funds/trusts statements, shares statements, etc)

[Page 1 of 6] **Annex F** [5]

HCMP No. [   ]/200[ ]

IN THE HIGH COURT OF THE
HONG KONG SPECIAL ADMINISTRATIVE REGION
COURT OF FIRST INSTANCE
MISCELLANEOUS PROCEEDINGS NO. [   ] OF 200 [ ]

IN THE MATTER OF Part II of the Mental Health Ordinance, Cap. 136 ("the Ordinance")

and

IN THE MATTER OF an alleged mentally incapacitated person [*Add initials of MIP*]

BEFORE [   ] IN CHAMBERS

ORDER

UPON hearing the Applicant's [solicitor/Counsel] and [*add initials of MIP*] being [*present/absent*]

AND THE COURT being satisfied that [*full name of MIP*] *[add initials of MIP]* is incapable, by reason of mental incapacity as defined in the Mental Health Ordinance, Cap. 136 of managing and administering [*his/her*] property and affairs.

IT IS ORDERED THAT

1.   [   ] be appointed Committee of the Estate of [add initials of MIP] in this matter with such powers only conferred by this Order or by any subsequent order, direction or authority of the Court.

[2.   As from the date hereof, so much as may be necessary is allowed for the maintenance and general benefit of [*add initials of MIP*] (including medical fees) and for such other purposes as the Court may from time to time direct and insofar as the net

---

5. See annex F to PD30.1 for the same order.

Annex F

income of [*add initials of MIP*] may be insufficient for those purposes, the Committee be entitled to resort to [*add initials of MIP*]'s capital.] [*if relevant*]

3. The Committee be authorized in the name and on behalf of [*add initials of MIP*] to give any necessary notices of withdrawal and to receive and to give a discharge for:-

    (a) all or any sums of money standing to the credit of [*add initials of MIP*] whether on current account, deposit account, fixed deposit or otherwise with, any licensed bank, restricted licensed bank, private bank, deposit-taking company, trust company doing business in Hong Kong or elsewhere whether the same be held in [*add initials of MIP*]'s own name or jointly with others and any investments held in the name of nominees in any financial institution;

    (b) all and any stock, shares, preferential shares and other similar assets held by [*add initials of MIP*] (whether alone or jointly with others) and any investments held in the name of nominees in any financial institution; and

    (c) all dividends, interest, payments from trusts, rent, licence fees, social security benefits and other income of whatever nature and from whatever source to which [*add initials of MIP*] is entitled (whether alone or jointly with others), or as may be directed by the Court.

4. The Committee be authorised to revoke in the name and on behalf of [*add initials of MIP*] all mandates and authorities given by [*add initials of MIP*] jointly with others to any licensed bank, restricted licensed bank, private bank, deposit-taking company, stockbroker, fund manager, investment adviser or manager and others doing business in Hong Kong or elsewhere.

5. The Committee be authorised to open and procure the opening of any safe deposit boxes in Hong Kong and elsewhere registered in the name of [add initials of MIP] (whether alone or jointly with others) and to transfer the contents to a safe deposit box (or boxes) in its own name which it is hereby authorised to open.

Annex F

[Page 3 of 6]

6. The Committee be empowered to deal with any money under its control belonging to [add initials of MIP] and any sums received by it under this order as follows:-

   (a) to pay the amount owing for the maintenance and general benefit of [*add initials of MIP*];

   (b) to pay any debts of [*add initials of MIP*];

   (c) to pay the costs of this application, as hereinafter provided; and

   [(d) to invest the surplus in accordance with the provisions of the Trustee Ordinance, Cap 29] [*if relevant*].

7. The Committee be empowered to open up a Committee bank account or accounts and security and/or investment accounts in the name of the Committee.

[8. The Committee be authorized from time to time to engage stock brokers, merchant bankers, tax advisers, accountants, solicitors and Counsel as it may deem necessary to advise on [*add initials of MIP*]'s assets and former assets (including assets and former assets owned jointly with others), and on any dealings or transfers of [*his/her*] assets and former assets (including assets and former assets owned jointly with others), and on the investment and management of [*add initials of MIP*] 's estate, and on the conduct of this Committee and generally in connection with or incidental to the discharge of the Committee's duties under this and any subsequent order herein and to pay from [*add initials of MIP*]'s estate the fees of all such advisers for so acting. The Committee is to report to this Court within 120 days hereof, or such other period as this Court may direct on the investment of [*add initials of MIP*]'s personal estate.] [*if relevant*]

9. The Committee be empowered to take such steps as it deems necessary or appropriate to ascertain and verify the extent of [*add initials of MIP*]'s assets in Hong Kong and elsewhere (including assets owned jointly with others) and be

[Page 4 of 6] **Annex F**

authorized to make such enquiries in the name of [*add initials of MIP*] and on [*his/her*] behalf as it considers appropriate for such purpose.

10.   The Committee to account to the Court as and when required provided that it shall do so at least once in each calendar year from the date of this order and provided also that the first of such accounts shall be for the period ending 31st December [   ] and such accounts shall be submitted to this Court within 120 days or such other period as the Court may direct from the end of such period.

11.   The Committee be empowered to take possession of all powers of attorney granted by [*add initials of MIP*] and all wills and any codicils thereto made by [*add initials of MIP*] and to make such enquiries on behalf of [*add initials of MIP*] in [*his/her*] name as it deems fit as to the terms of such powers of attorney, wills and codicils, [*his/her*] instructions in relation thereto, any advice (including legal advice) given to [*his/her*] in relation thereto and the circumstances in which such powers of attorney, wills and codicils were made.

12.   Any securities and any title deeds belonging to [*add initials of MIP*] are to be deposited in the name of the Committee in a safe deposit box and to remain so deposited subject to the directions of the Court.

13.   The costs of the Applicant and [*his/her*] solicitors and of the Committee of and incidental to and consequential upon this application are fixed pursuant to Order 62 Rule 9(4)(b) at $ and the Committee is to pay the same from [*add initials of MIP*]'s assets.

14.   [The Committee be remunerated for its services in accordance with the terms set out in its letter to the Applicant's Solicitors dated [   ] which is attached to the Certificate of Family and Property filed in these proceedings, subject to such further order in relation thereto as may hereinafter be made.] [*if relevant, usually the court will not allow remuneration for next of kin who acts as the Committee*]

15.   [The Committee to act without providing security which is to be dispensed with.]

[Page 5 of 6] **Annex F**

16.	The Committee be at liberty to instruct solicitors and Counsel in Hong Kong and abroad at the expense of [*add initials of MIP*] generally in connection with or incidental to the discharge of its duties under this and any subsequent order herein. [*if relevant*]

17.	There be liberty to apply.

[18.	No information shall be published in relation to these proceedings or this and any subsequent order in these proceedings save as may be necessary for the purpose of carrying the same into effect and implementing the terms thereof or as may be expressly authorised by further order of this Court.]

[19.	The Committee to report on enquiries of [*add initials of MIP*]'s relatives including the following:-
	[	*please complete*	]	]

[20.	Add Orders with regard to for example :

	(a)	Conducting legal proceedings;
	(b)	the sale of property or leases for more than 3 years;
	(c)	the possession of movable property not deposited in a safe deposit box.

	[	*please complete*	]	]

Dated this [	] day of [	] 200 [ ]

REGISTRAR

[Page 6 of 6] **Annex F**

HCMP No.[   ]/ 200 [   ]

IN THE HIGH COURT OF THE
HONG KONG SPECIAL ADMINISTRATIVE REGION
COURT OF FIRST INSTANCE
MISCELLANEOUS PROCEEDINGS NO. [   ] OF 200[   ]

IN THE MATTER OF Part II of the Mental Health Ordinance, Cap. 136 ("the Ordinance")

and

IN THE MATTER OF an alleged mentally incapacitated person [*Add initials of MIP*]

- -

ORDER

- -

Filed this [   ] day of [   ] 200 [   ]

Part III

7
Other Planning Tools: Enduring Power of Attorney, Advance Directive, and Continuing Power of Attorney

In Chapter 4, the concept of **Mental Capacity** was introduced. You may recall that Capacity in general terms is the mental ability to make a particular decision, eg whether to accept or refuse medical treatment, how to spend one's money on daily matters and/or more complex financial decisions including investment, wealth and succession planning, etc.

As mentioned, there are different levels of Capacity required in making a will, enduring power of attorney or advance directives and there are specialist doctors like psychiatrists who are trained to assess a person's mental capacity to manage and administer his or her property and affairs.

In this chapter, I will highlight other planning tools such as enduring power of attorney, advance directives, and the emerging continuing power of attorney which a person may consider making during his lifetime when he or she still has Mental Capacity to do so.

Enduring Power of Attorney (EPA)

An EPA is a document which allows a person making the EPA (**Donor**) to appoint attorneys (**Attorney**) and to give directions as to his or her affairs in the subsequent event that the Donor becomes mentally incapacitated.[1]

The current EPA regime is governed by the Enduring Powers of Attorney Ordinance (Cap 501) (**EPAO**). EPAs are limited to arrangements of the Donor's property and financial affairs.[2]

Characteristics of an EPA

An EPA must be in a prescribed form, according to section 3 of the EPAO.

---

1. Section 4 of the EPAO.
2. Section 8(1) of the EPAO.

Unless it is specified to take effect on a later date or upon a certain event, an EPA takes effect on the date of execution.[3]

An EPA will continue to be valid even after the Donor becomes mentally incapacitated, which means the Attorney can continue to manage the affairs of the Donor after the Donor becomes mentally incapacitated.

In contrast, an ordinary power of attorney will expire upon the Donor becoming mentally incapacitated.[4]

Execution of an EPA

In executing the EPA, the Donor must sign the EPA before a registered medical practitioner and a solicitor. The EPA must be signed before the solicitor either at the same time when it is signed before a medical practitioner or within 28 days of the signing before a medical practitioner.[5]

The solicitor must certify that:[6]

1. the Donor appears to be mentally capable;
2. the EPA was signed in the presence of the solicitor; and
3. the Donor signed the EPA voluntarily.

The medical practitioner must certify that:[7]

1. he or she is satisfied that the Donor is mentally capable;
2. the EPA was signed in the presence of the medical practitioner; and
3. the Donor signed the EPA voluntarily.

The Attorney must also sign the EPA.[8] Although the Attorney does not necessarily have to sign the EPA at the same time as the Donor, in practice it is often done simultaneously.[9]

---

3. Section 10 of the EPAO.
4. Section 4 of the EPAO.
5. Section 5(2)(a) of the EPAO; see also para 11 of Form 1 under Sch 1 to the Enduring Powers of Attorney (Prescribed Form) Regulation (Cap 501A) (**EPAR**) (for sole Attorneys) and para 12 of Form 2 under Sch 2 to the EPAR.
6. Section 5(2)(d) of the EPAO; see also para 11 of Form 1 under Sch 1 and para 12 of Form 2 under Sch 2 to the EPAR.
7. Section 5(2)(e) of the EPAO; see also para 11 of Form 1 under Sch 1 to the EPAR (for sole Attorneys) and para 12 of Form 2 under Sch 2 to the EPAR (for joint Attorneys).
8. Section 5(2)(c) of the EPAO.
9. Section 3 of the EPAO.

The registered medical practitioner and the solicitor must not be the same person as the Attorney and must not be the spouse of a person related by blood or marriage to the Donor or the Attorney.[10]

The requirements and duties of an attorney

An Attorney of an EPA must be at least 18 years old and not bankrupt or mentally incapable. Alternatively, an Attorney can be a trust corporation.[11]

Since the powers of the Attorney of an EPA can be very wide, one must be careful when choosing an Attorney and must specify clearly the scope and restrictions of the power. The Donor must not give the Attorney general authority over all his or her property and financial affairs, otherwise the EPA will not be valid.[12]

The Attorney has a duty to apply to the Registrar of the High Court to register the EPA when the Donor is, or is becoming, mentally incapable.[13]

The Attorney owes a fiduciary duty to the Donor and has a duty to:[14]

1. exercise his or her powers honestly and with due diligence;
2. keep proper accounts and records;
3. not enter into any transaction where a conflict of interest would arise with the Donor; and
4. not mix the property of the Donor with other property.

The scope and restrictions of an attorney

An EPA must specify the particular matters in relation to which the Attorney has authority to act,[15] for example:[16]

1. collecting any income due to the Donor;
2. collecting any capital due to the Donor;
3. selling any of the Donor's movable property;
4. selling, leasing or surrendering the Donor's home of any of his or her immovable property;
5. spending any of the Donor's income; and
6. spending any of the Donor's capital.

---

10. Section 5(2)(aa) of the EPAO.
11. Section 6 of the EPAO.
12. See, for example, paras 6, 7 and 10 of Form 1 under Sch 1 (for sole Attorneys) and paras 6, 7, and 11 of Form 2 under Sch 2 (for joint Attorneys) to the EPAR.
13. See Clause 1 of Part B of the Form of EPA under Form 1 of Sch 1 to the EPAR.
14. Section 12 of the EPAO.
15. Section 8 of the EPAO.
16. Clause 2 of Part A of the Form of EPA under Form 1 of Sch 1 to the EPAR.

The Donor can also list out specific property or financial affairs that he or she wants the Attorney to deal with.

If the Donor would like to restrict the Attorney from acting on his or her behalf, unless the Attorney believes that the Donor is mentally incapacitated, the Donor can specify such a restriction in the EPA.[17] The Donor can also request the Attorney to notify him or her before the Attorney applies for registration of the EPA.[18]

The Attorney may only make gifts of a seasonal nature or at a birthday or marriage anniversary to persons (including the Attorney) who are connected with the Donor and any charity, which the Donor might be expected to make gifts to.[19] Such gifts must be reasonable in all circumstances, in particular in relation to the Donor's estate.[20] The Attorney may also benefit himself or other persons if the Donor might be expected to do so.[21]

If the Donor wishes to appoint only one Attorney, Form 1 should be used. If the Donor wishes to appoint more than one Attorney, Form 2 should be used. Samples of these forms can be found at the end of this chapter.

The Interplay between the EPA Regime and Committee Regime

So, one may ask, if I have prepared an EPA authorizing my Attorney to handle my property and financial affairs, do I still need a Committee to be appointed by the court on my behalf when I subsequently become mentally incapacitated?

As mentioned above, you cannot give a general authority over all your property and financial affairs in the EPA. If you do, your EPA will be invalid.

Since the authority conferred to the Attorney by an EPA is limited to financial and property matters which must be specified, eg collecting income due to you or selling your landed property, etc, there may well be other matters which are not covered by the EPA and may need to be dealt with by a court-appointed Committee.

The powers conferred to the Committee under section 11 of the MHO are much wider, and the court can decide whether the residual matters that were left out of the EPA would go beyond the realm of the EPA's powers.

The court, in considering the appointment of a Committee where there is an existing EPA, will ensure that there will be no conflict or inconsistency between the powers given to the Committee and the powers conferred to the Attorney in the EPA.

---

17. Clause 3 of Part A of the Form of EPA under Form 1 of Sch 1 to the EPAR.
18. Clause 4 of Part A of the Form of EPA under Form 1 of Sch 1 to the EPAR.
19. Section 8(3)(c) of the EPAO.
20. Section 8(4) of the EPAO.
21. Section 8(3)(b) of the EPAO.

In situations where serious allegations are made about the conduct of the Attorney under an EPA in respect of the actual management of the MIP's affairs, the court may consider it in the best interests of the MIP to appoint a Committee to manage the financial affairs of the MIP with powers of investigation against the conduct of the Attorney.[22]

In the judgment of *Re C v B* dated 2 March 2018, Mr Justice Lok clearly explained the interplay between the EPA regime and the Part II Committee regime and the considerations taken into account when exercising judicial discretion against the appointment of a Part II Committee where there is already an EPA in place. You may refer to this judgment if you are interested in the development of this area of law.

Thus, it is possible that in certain complex cases it may be necessary for the court to appoint a Committee on behalf of a mentally incapacitated person, even where there is an EPA in place, to cover the residual matters which have been omitted from the EPA or fall outside the realm of the EPA. However, in cases where the EPA adequately covers the financial affairs of the MIP, a court appointed Committee will not be necessary.

Advance Directive (AD)

A mentally competent and properly-informed adult patient aged 18 or above (**Donor**) can give directions in an AD in relation to the health care and/or medical treatment he or she would like to receive in the future when he or she becomes mentally incapacitated.[23] However, ADs do not have legal status in Hong Kong.[24] While it is arguable that an AD is valid and legally binding under the common law, there is no legislation on this. Yet a person can still make an AD as to his or her medical treatment, and such wishes will be recognized unless the AD is challenged.[25]

The Hospital Authority (**HA**) has designed an AD form (which can be found at the end of this chapter) for use by its patients addressing life-sustaining treatment in the following scenarios:[26]

---

22. See the judgment of Lok J in *Re C v B*, unrep., HCMH No 19 of 2016 (2 March 2018).
23. See paras 3 and 6 of the "Introduction of the Concept of Advance Directives in Hong Kong Consultation Paper", published by the Food and Health Bureau of the Hong Kong government (**Advance Directives Consultation Paper**).
24. See para 12 of the Advance Directives Consultation Paper.
25. See "Substitute Decision-making and Advance Directives in Relation to Medical Treatment", published by The Law Reform Commission of Hong Kong, August 2006, para 8.33; and para 12 of the Advance Directives Consultation Paper.
26. See "Public Education Material—Advance Care Planning / Advance Directive / Do Not Attempt CPR (2016)" published by the HA, available at http://www.ha.org.hk/haho/ho/psrm/Public_education2.pdf.

1. for terminally-ill patients where the application of life-sustaining treatment would only serve to postpone the moment of death;
2. for patients in a persistent vegetative state or a state of irreversible coma; and
3. for patients under other end-stage irreversible life-limiting condition.

The HA also has a prescribed form for revoking an AD.[27]

While the HA has designed the AD form for use by its patients to minimize distress or indignity which they may suffer when they are terminally ill or in a persistent vegetative state or other end-stage irreversible condition, it has been reported that the HA has, in certain cases, declined to register patients' ADs regarding life-sustaining treatment in their medical records.[28]

Continuing Powers of Attorney (CPA)

Due to the limitations of EPAs and ADs, the Department of Justice proposed a Continuing Powers of Attorney Bill for a new CPA regime in December 2017 (**CPA Bill**). The new regime extends CPAs to cover directions in relation to the Donor's personal care as well as financial matters.[29] A CPA, similar to an EPA, also survives the subsequent mental incapacity of the Donor.[30]

However, the Attorney may only act in relation to the Donor's personal care if the Attorney has reasonable grounds to believe that the Donor is mentally incapable of deciding on his or her own personal care matters.[31]

Personal care matters refer to the Donor's welfare matters other than his financial matters.[32] Examples of personal care matters include:[33]

1. where the Donor lives;
2. whom the Donor lives with;

---

27. See the Forms under Healthcare Professionals > Professional Knowledge > Clinical Ethics > "Guidance for HA Clinicians on Advance Directives in Adults (2016)", available at www.ha.org.hk.
28. See "公院醫生拒收病人瀕死指示" [A doctor in public hospital refuses to register the advance directive of a patient], *Apple Daily*, 12 December 2017.
29. Clause 3 of the CPA Bill; and para 15 of the "Consultation Paper on the Continuing Powers of Attorney Bill", published by the Department of Justice in December 2017.
30. Clause 2 of the CPA Bill.
31. Clause 3(5) of the CPA Bill.
32. Clause 2 of the CPA Bill.
33. Clause 6 of the CPA Bill.

3. the Donor's daily dress and diet;
4. whether, if so where, the Donor goes on holiday;
5. whether to refuse any specific individual to have access to, or contact with, the Donor;
6. legal matters relating to the Donor's personal care; and
7. matters relating to the Donor's healthcare.

Restrictions on the Attorney's power include decisions to give, refuse or withdraw life-sustaining treatment for the Donor or to make, vary or revoke an AD of the Donor.[34]

An Attorney of a CPA must be at least 18 years of age and possess mental capacity. If the CPA is only in relation to financial matters, it can be a trust corporation.[35]

A CPA must be in prescribed form.[36] The prescribed form is based on the form under section 3(1) and (2) of the EPAO.[37]

The proposed nature and scope of the CPA Bill appear to be much wider than the EPA and guardianship regimes. Whilst the CPA is a better planning tool for the Donor as it covers directions in relation to the Donor's personal care as well as financial matters that survive the Donor's mental incapacity, caution must be taken to prevent any potential abuse by the Attorney.

Thus, a consolidated statutory body to govern and supervise Attorneys is needed to ensure that the persons under guardianship and/or Donors are safe and protected from abuse and neglect, and a referral system is in place in the event of danger to the health and wellbeing of persons under guardianship and/or Donors.

---

34. Clauses 4 and 5 of the CPA Bill.
35. Clause 8 of the CPA Bill.
36. Clauses 24 and 25 of the CPA Bill.
37. See para 26 of the Consultation Paper on the Continuing Powers of Attorney Bill, published by the Department of Justice in December 2017.

ENDURING POWER OF ATTORNEY

(Enduring Powers of Attorney Ordinance – CAP.501)

FORM 1

[section 1A]

Information you must read

1. This form is a legal document that allows you to create an enduring power of attorney (***EPA***). An EPA enables you to authorize another person (***your attorney***) to act on your behalf in relation to your property and financial affairs. You must use this form if you intend to appoint only one attorney. If you become mentally incapable, your attorney will be able to make decisions for you after your attorney has registered this form with the Registrar of the High Court.

2. (Repealed 13 of 2013 s. 59)

3. You must complete Part A.

4. **Paragraph 1 of Part A:** You must include the name and address of the person you wish to appoint as your attorney at paragraph 1 of Part A. The person you appoint as your attorney must be over 18 years of age and must not be bankrupt or mentally incapable. Your attorney does not have to be a solicitor. Your attorney must complete Part B and sign this form in the presence of a witness.

5. **Paragraph 2 of Part A:** You cannot give your attorney a general authority over all your property and financial affairs. If you do, your EPA will not be valid. Instead, you must specify at paragraph 2 of Part A what you authorize your attorney to do with your property and financial affairs, or the particular property or financial affairs for which you have given your attorney authority to act. For example, you may decide to give your attorney authority only for a particular bank account, or a particular piece of property.

6. **Paragraph 3 of Part A:** You may include any restrictions you like on the authority you give to your attorney. For example, you may include a restriction that your attorney must not act on your behalf until your attorney has reason to believe that you are becoming mentally incapable, or that your attorney must not enter into a contract

without first seeking legal advice if its value exceeds a specified amount. You should set out these restrictions at paragraph 3 of Part A.

7. Unless you include a restriction preventing it, your attorney will be able to use any of your money or property to make any provision which you might be expected to make yourself for the needs of your attorney or the needs of other persons. Your attorney will be able to use your money to make gifts, but only for reasonable amounts in relation to the value of your money and property.

8. Your attorney may recover out-of-pocket expenses for acting as your attorney. If your attorney is a professional person, such as an accountant or a solicitor, your attorney may charge for any professional services provided when acting as your attorney.

9. If your attorney has reason to believe that you are, or are becoming, mentally incapable of managing your affairs, your attorney must apply to the Registrar of the High Court to register this EPA. Registration will allow your attorney to make decisions for you after you have become mentally incapable.

10. **Paragraph 4 of Part A:** If you would like to be notified before your attorney applies to the Registrar of the High Court to register this EPA, or if you would like other persons to be notified, you must include the names and addresses of the persons to be notified at paragraph 4 of Part A. You can include up to 2 persons to be notified in addition to yourself. If your attorney does not notify you or the persons you have nominated, that does not prevent the registration of your EPA or make it invalid. However, in any legal proceedings relating to the EPA the court may, if it considers it appropriate, draw an adverse inference from the failure to notify you or the nominated persons.

11. **Paragraphs 7, 9 and 10 of Part A:** You must sign this form at paragraph 7 of Part A and fill in the names and addresses of the registered medical practitioner and the solicitor who are present when you sign. If you do not sign in the presence of both the registered medical practitioner and the solicitor at the same time, you must sign the form in the presence of the solicitor no later than 28 days after the date on which you sign in the presence of the registered medical practitioner. The registered medical practitioner and the solicitor will need to complete the certificates at paragraphs 9 and 10 of Part A respectively to certify that you are mentally capable when you sign this form.

12. **Paragraph 8 of Part A:** If you are physically incapable of signing this form yourself, you can direct someone else to sign on your behalf. In this case, paragraph 8 of Part A must be completed and that person must sign at that paragraph in your presence and in the presence of the registered medical practitioner and the solicitor. The person signing on your behalf must not be your attorney, the spouse of your attorney, the registered medical practitioner or the solicitor before whom the instrument is signed or the spouse of the registered medical practitioner or the solicitor.

13. This form takes effect as an EPA in accordance with section 10 of the Enduring Powers of Attorney Ordinance (Cap 501) when it is signed by you or the person signing on your behalf and under your direction before the solicitor. You should note that unless and until this form is so signed, it has no effect either as an EPA or an ordinary power of attorney. However, if you wish, you may choose a later date or later event, on which the EPA will take effect. In such case you must specify this later date or event in paragraph 5 of Part A.

Form of enduring power of attorney (for appointment of only one attorney)

Part A

*[This Part must be completed by the person appointing the attorney **(the donor)**, except for paragraphs 9 and 10, which must be completed by a registered medical practitioner and a solicitor respectively. You should read the explanatory information given under the heading* "**Information you must read**" *before you fill it in. Do not sign this form unless you understand what it means.]*

1. **Appointment of attorney by donor**

I, *[your name here]* .... ,
holder of *[your identification document here]* .... ,
of *[your address here]* ....
....
appoint *[your attorney's name here]* ....
holder of *[identification document here]* .... ,
of *[your attorney's address here]* ....
....

to be my attorney under the Enduring Powers of Attorney Ordinance (Cap 501).

2. **Attorney's authority**

[You must specify what you authorize your attorney to do. You cannot give a general authority over all your property and financial affairs. ***If you do, your EPA will not be valid.*** *You can **either** specify at subparagraph (1) what you authorize your attorney to do by ticking any or all of the appropriate boxes,* ***or*** *tick no box, in which case you must list at subparagraph (2) the particular property or financial affairs for which you have given your attorney authority to act. If you have ticked any or all the boxes at subparagraph (1), you may still list at subparagraph (2) any particular property or financial affairs in relation to which you have given your attorney authority to act. You must not make no ticks at subparagraph (1)* ***and*** *list no property at subparagraph (2).]*

(1) My attorney has authority to act on my behalf:

☐ (a) to collect any income due to me;
☐ (b) to collect any capital due to me;
☐ (c) to sell any of my movable property;
☐ (d) to sell, lease or surrender my home or any of my immovable property;
☐ (e) to spend any of my income;
☐ (f) to spend any of my capital. (13 of 2013 s. 59)
☐ (g) (Repealed 13 of 2013 s. 59)

(2) My attorney has authority to act on my behalf in respect of the following property or financial affairs: *[If you want your attorney to act for you only in relation to some of your property or financial affairs, you must list them here.]*

....
....
....
....

3. **Restrictions on attorney**

This enduring power of attorney is subject to the following conditions and restrictions:

[If you want to put conditions or restrictions on the way your attorney exercises any powers, you must list them here. For example, you may include a restriction that your attorney must not act on your behalf until your attorney has reason to believe that you are becoming mentally incapable. If you do not want to impose any conditions or restrictions, you must delete this paragraph.]

....
....
....

4. Notification of named persons

*[If you do not want anyone (including yourself) to be notified of the application for the registration of this EPA, you must delete subparagraphs (1) **and** (2).]*

(1) My attorney must notify me before applying for the registration of this enduring power of attorney. *[If you do not want to be notified, you must delete this subparagraph.]*

(2) My attorney must notify the following persons before applying for the registration of this enduring power of attorney. *[Fill in the names and addresses of up to 2 persons (other than yourself) to be notified. If you do not want other persons to be notified, you must delete this subparagraph.]*

Name: ....
Address: ....
Name: ....
Address: ....

5. Commencement of EPA

[This EPA takes effect on the date it is signed before the solicitor in paragraph 7 or 8 below. If you want to specify a later date or later event on which this EPA will take effect, please fill in the gap in the sentence marked with an asterisk below. Delete that sentence if you wish this EPA to take effect on the date it is signed before the solicitor.]

*This EPA takes effect on ....
.... (insert a later date or event).

6. Power to continue

I intend this enduring power of attorney to continue even if I become mentally incapable.

7. Signatures

Signed by me as a deed *[sign here]* ....
on *[date]* ....
in the presence of *[name and address of registered medical practitioner]* ....
....
....

Signed by me as a deed *[sign here]* ....
on *[date]* ....
in the presence of *[name and address of solicitor]* ....
....
....

8. *[If you are physically incapable of signing this form and you direct someone else to sign on your behalf, that person must sign here and paragraph 7 must be deleted.]*

This enduring power of attorney has been signed by *[name of person signing on your behalf]*
....
holder of *[identification document]* .... ,
of *[address of person signing on your behalf]* ....
....
under the direction and in the presence of the donor.

Signed as a deed *[signature of person signing on your behalf]* ....
....
on *[date]* ....
in the presence of the donor and *[name and address of registered medical practitioner]* ....
....

....

Signed as a deed *[signature of person signing on your behalf]* ....

....

on *[date]* ....

in the presence of the donor and *[name and address of solicitor]* ....

....

....

9. Certificate by registered medical practitioner

I certify that:

(a) I am satisfied that the donor is mentally capable in terms of section 2 of the Enduring Powers of Attorney Ordinance (Cap 501); and

(b) this form was signed by the donor in my presence and the donor acknowledged signing it voluntarily. *[If someone else signs this form on the donor's behalf, this statement must be deleted.]*

(c) this form was signed, in the presence of the donor and me, by *[name of person signing on donor's behalf]* ....

....

on behalf and under the direction of the donor. *[If the donor signs this form, this statement must be deleted.]*

Signed by registered medical practitioner ....

on *[date]* ....

10. Certificate by solicitor

I certify that:

(a) the donor appears to be mentally capable in terms of section 2 of the Enduring Powers of Attorney Ordinance (Cap 501); and

(b) this form was signed by the donor in my presence and the donor acknowledged signing it voluntarily. *[If someone else signs this form on the donor's behalf, this statement must be deleted.]*

(c) this form was signed, in the presence of the donor and me, by *[name of person signing on donor's behalf]* ....

on behalf and under the direction of the donor. *[If the donor signs this form, this statement must be deleted.]*

Signed by solicitor ....
on *[date]* ....

Part B

[This Part must be completed by the attorney.]

1. I understand that I have a duty to apply to the Registrar of the High Court to register this form under the Enduring Powers of Attorney Ordinance (Cap 501) when the donor is, or is becoming, mentally incapable.

2. I also understand my limited power to use the donor's property to benefit persons other than the donor as provided in section 8(3) and (4) of that Ordinance and also my duties and liabilities under section 12 of that Ordinance

3. Signed by me as a deed *[signature of attorney]* ....
on *[date]* ....
in the presence of *[signature and name and address of witness, who must not be the donor]*
....
....
....

(Schedule 1 replaced 25 of 2011 s. 13)

ENDURING POWER OF ATTORNEY

(Enduring Powers of Attorney Ordinance – CAP.501)

FORM 2

[section 1A]

Information you must read

1. This form is a legal document that allows you to create an enduring power of attorney (***EPA***). An EPA enables you to authorize another person to act on your behalf in relation to your property and financial affairs. You must use this form if you intend to appoint more than one person to act on your behalf. If you become mentally incapable, the persons you have appointed (***your attorneys***) will be able to make decisions for you after they have registered this form with the Registrar of the High Court.

2. (Repealed 13 of 2013 s. 60)

3. **Paragraph 2 of Part A:** You must decide whether your attorneys are to act—

> (a) jointly (that is, they must all act together and cannot act separately); or
> (b) jointly and severally (that is, they can all act together but they can also act separately if they wish).

You must indicate your decision at paragraph 2 of Part A. You should note that if your attorneys are to act jointly, on the bankruptcy or death of any one of them this power of attorney becomes revoked under law.

4. You must complete Part A.

5. **Paragraph 1 of Part A:** You must include the names and addresses of the persons you wish to appoint as your attorneys at paragraph 1 of Part A. The persons you appoint as your attorneys must be over 18 years of age and must not be bankrupt or mentally incapable. Your attorneys do not have to be solicitors. Your attorneys must complete Part B and each of them must sign this form in the presence of a witness.

Other Planning Tools

6. **Paragraph 3 of Part A:** You cannot give your attorneys a general authority over all your property and financial affairs. If you do, your EPA will not be valid. Instead, you must specify at paragraph 3 of Part A what you authorize your attorneys to do with your property and financial affairs, or the particular property or financial affairs for which you have given your attorneys authority to act. For example, you may decide to give your attorneys authority only for a particular bank account, or a particular piece of property.

7. **Paragraph 4 of Part A:** You may include any restrictions you like on the authority you give to your attorneys. For example, you may include a restriction that your attorneys must not act on your behalf until they have reason to believe that you are becoming mentally incapable, or that your attorneys must not enter into a contract without first seeking legal advice if its value exceeds a specified amount. You should set out these restrictions at paragraph 4 of Part A.

8. Unless you include a restriction preventing it, your attorneys will be able to use any of your money or property to make any provision which you might be expected to make yourself for the needs of your attorneys or the needs of other persons. Your attorneys will be able to use your money to make gifts, but only for reasonable amounts in relation to the value of your money and property.

9. Your attorneys may recover out-of-pocket expenses for acting as your attorneys. If any of your attorneys is a professional person, such as an accountant or a solicitor, that attorney may charge for any professional services provided when acting as your attorney.

10. If your attorneys have reason to believe that you are, or are becoming, mentally incapable of managing your affairs, they must apply to the Registrar of the High Court to register this EPA. Registration will allow your attorneys to make decisions for you after you have become mentally incapable.

11. **Paragraph 5 of Part A:** If you would like to be notified before your attorneys apply to the Registrar of the High Court to register this EPA, or if you would like other persons to be notified, you must include the names and addresses of the persons to be notified at paragraph 5 of Part A. If you have decided that your attorneys may act separately, you may also nominate any of your attorneys not joining in the application to be notified. You can include up to 2 persons to be notified in addition to yourself and any attorney not joining in the application. If your attorneys do not notify

you or the persons you have nominated, that does not prevent the registration of your EPA or make it invalid. However, in any legal proceedings relating to the EPA the court may, if it considers it appropriate, draw an adverse inference from the failure to notify you or the nominated persons.

12. **Paragraphs 8, 10 and 11 of Part A:** You must sign this form at paragraph 8 of Part A and fill in the names and addresses of the registered medical practitioner and the solicitor who are present when you sign. If you do not sign in the presence of both the registered medical practitioner and the solicitor at the same time, you must sign the form in the presence of the solicitor no later than 28 days after the date on which you sign in the presence of the registered medical practitioner. The registered medical practitioner and the solicitor will need to complete the certificates at paragraphs 10 and 11 of Part A respectively to certify that you are mentally capable when you sign this form.

13. **Paragraph 9 of Part A:** If you are physically incapable of signing this form yourself, you can direct someone else to sign on your behalf. In this case, paragraph 9 of Part A must be completed and that person must sign at that paragraph in your presence and in the presence of the registered medical practitioner and the solicitor. The person signing on your behalf must not be one of your attorneys, the spouse of any one of your attorneys, the registered medical practitioner or the solicitor before whom the instrument is signed or the spouse of the registered medical practitioner or the solicitor.

14. This form takes effect as an EPA in accordance with section 10 of the Enduring Powers of Attorney Ordinance (Cap 501) when it is signed by you or the person signing on your behalf and under your direction before the solicitor. You should note that unless and until this form is so signed, it has no effect either as an EPA or an ordinary power of attorney.

However, if you wish, you may choose a later date or later event, on which the EPA will take effect. In such case you must specify this later date or event in paragraph 6 of Part A.

Form of enduring power of attorney (for appointment of more than one attorney)

Part A

Other Planning Tools

*[This Part must be completed by the person appointing the attorneys **(the donor)**, except for paragraphs 10 and 11, which must be completed by a registered medical practitioner and a solicitor respectively. You should read the explanatory information given under the heading **"Information you must read"** before you fill it in. Do not sign this form unless you understand what it means.]*

1. **Appointment of attorneys by donor**

I, *[your name here]* .... ,
holder of *[your identification document here]* .... ,
of *[your address here]* ....
....

appoint

    (a) *[your attorney's name here]* ....
        holder of *[identification document here]* .... ,
        of *[your attorney's address here]* ....
        .... ;
    and

    (b) *[your attorney's name here]* ....
        holder of *[identification document here]* .... ,
        of *[your attorney's address here]* ....
        .... ;

[If you appoint more than 2 attorneys, please add additional subparagraph(s) similar to subparagraphs (a) and (b).]

to be my attorneys under the Enduring Powers of Attorney Ordinance (Cap 501).

2. **Whether attorneys must act jointly**

*[You must decide whether your attorneys are to act (a) jointly; **or** (b) jointly and severally. See paragraph 3 under the heading **"Information you must read"** and delete either (a) or (b) from the statement below. **If you do not, your EPA will not be valid.**]*

My attorneys appointed under paragraph 1 are to act—

(a) jointly.

or

(b) jointly and severally.

3. **Attorneys' authority**

[You must specify what you authorize your attorneys to do. You cannot give a general authority over all your property and financial affairs. **If you do, your EPA will not be valid.** *You can* **either** *specify at subparagraph (1) what you authorize your attorneys to do by ticking any or all of the appropriate boxes,* **or** *tick no box, in which case you must list at subparagraph (2) the particular property or financial affairs for which you have given your attorneys authority to act. If you have ticked any or all the boxes at subparagraph (1), you may still list at subparagraph (2) any particular property or financial affairs in relation to which you have given your attorneys authority to act. You must not make no ticks at subparagraph (1)* **and** *list no property at subparagraph (2).]*

(1) My attorneys have authority to act on my behalf:

☐ (a) to collect any income due to me;
☐ (b) to collect any capital due to me;
☐ (c) to sell any of my movable property;
☐ (d) to sell, lease or surrender my home or any of my immovable property;
☐ (e) to spend any of my income;
☐ (f) to spend any of my capital. (13 of 2013 s. 60)
☐ (g) (Repealed 13 of 2013 s. 60)

(2) My attorneys have authority to act on my behalf in respect of the following property or financial affairs: *[If you want your attorneys to act for you only in relation to some of your property or financial affairs, you must list them here.]*

....
....
....
....

4. Restrictions on attorneys

This enduring power of attorney is subject to the following conditions and restrictions:
[If you want to put conditions or restrictions on the way your attorneys exercise any powers, you must list them here. For example, you may include a restriction that your attorneys must not act on your behalf until they have reason to believe that you are becoming mentally incapable. If you do not want to impose any conditions or restrictions, you must delete this paragraph.]

....
....
....

5. Notification of named persons

*[If you do not want anyone (including yourself) to be notified of the application for the registration of this EPA, you must delete subparagraphs (1), (2) **and** (3).]*

(1) My attorneys must notify me before applying for the registration of this enduring power of attorney. *[If you do not want to be notified, you must delete this subparagraph.]*

(2) Any attorney applying for the registration of this enduring power of attorney must, before the application is made, notify any attorney not joining in the application. *[If you decide that your attorneys may act separately and you do not require any attorney applying for the registration of this EPA to notify any attorney not joining in the application, you must delete this subparagraph.]*

(3) My attorneys must notify the following persons before applying for the registration of this enduring power of attorney. *[Fill in the names and addresses of up to 2 persons (other than yourself or any of your attorneys) to be notified. If you do not want other persons to be notified, you must delete this subparagraph.]*

Name: ....
Address: ....
Name: ....
Address: ....

6. Commencement of EPA

[This EPA takes effect on the date it is signed before the solicitor in paragraph 8 or 9 below. If you want to specify a later date or later event on which this EPA will take effect, please fill in the gap in the sentence marked with an asterisk below. Delete that sentence if you wish this EPA to take effect on the date it is signed before the solicitor.]

*This EPA takes effect on ....

.... (insert a later date or event).

7. Power to continue

I intend this enduring power of attorney to continue even if I become mentally incapable.

8. Signatures

Signed by me as a deed *[sign here]* ....
on *[date]* ....
in the presence of *[name and address of registered medical practitioner]* ....
....
....

Signed by me as a deed *[sign here]* ....
on *[date]* ....
in the presence of *[name and address of solicitor]* ....
....
....

9. *[If you are physically incapable of signing this form and you direct someone else to sign on your behalf, that person must sign here and paragraph 8 must be deleted.]*

This enduring power of attorney has been signed by *[name of person signing on your behalf]*

....

Other Planning Tools

holder of *[identification document here]* .... ,
of *[address of person signing on your behalf]* ....
....
under the direction and in the presence of the donor.

Signed as a deed *[signature of person signing on your behalf]* ....
....
on *[date]* ....
in the presence of the donor and *[name and address of registered medical practitioner]* ....
....
....

Signed as a deed *[signature of person signing on your behalf]* ....
....
on *[date]* ....
in the presence of the donor and *[name and address of solicitor]* ....
....
....

10. Certificate by registered medical practitioner

I certify that:

> (a) I am satisfied that the donor is mentally capable in terms of section 2 of the Enduring Powers of Attorney Ordinance (Cap 501); and
> (b) this form was signed by the donor in my presence and the donor acknowledged signing it voluntarily. *[If someone else signs this form on the donor's behalf, this statement must be deleted.]*
> (c) this form was signed, in the presence of the donor and me, by *[name of person signing on donor's behalf]* ....
> ....
> on behalf and under the direction of the donor. *[If the donor signs this form, this statement must be deleted.]*

Signed by registered medical practitioner ....
on *[date]* ....

11. Certificate by solicitor

I certify that:

(a) the donor appears to be mentally capable in terms of section 2 of the Enduring Powers of Attorney Ordinance (Cap 501); and

(b) this form was signed by the donor in my presence and the donor acknowledged signing it voluntarily. *[If someone else signs this form on the donor's behalf, this statement must be deleted.]*

(c) this form was signed, in the presence of the donor and me, by *[name of person signing on donor's behalf]* ....

....

on behalf and under the direction of the donor. *[If the donor signs this form, this statement must be deleted.]*

Signed by solicitor ....
on *[date]* ....

Part B

[This Part must be completed by the attorneys. If you decide that your attorneys may act separately, then at least one of the attorneys appointed must sign this form for it to take effect as an EPA. An attorney will have the functions of an attorney under this EPA only if that attorney has signed this form.]

1. We understand that we have a duty to apply to the Registrar of the High Court to register this form under the Enduring Powers of Attorney Ordinance (Cap 501) when the donor is, or is becoming, mentally incapable.

2. We also understand our limited power to use the donor's property to benefit persons other than the donor as provided in section 8(3) and (4) of that Ordinance and also our duties and liabilities under section 12 of that Ordinance.

3. Signed as a deed—

(a) by *[signature and name of attorney]* ....

....

on *[date]* ....

in the presence of *[signature and name and address of witness, who must not be the donor or another attorney of the donor]* ....

....

....

.... ;

and

(b) by *[signature and name of attorney]* ....

....

on *[date]* ....
in the presence of *[signature and name and address of witness, who must not be the donor or another attorney of the donor]* ....

....

....

....

[If you appoint more than 2 attorneys, please add additional subparagraph(s) similar to subparagraphs (a) and (b).]

(Schedule 2 added 25 of 2011 s. 14)

Appendix 1

HOSPITAL AUTHORITY

ADVANCE DIRECTIVE[1]

Please Use Block Letter or Affix Label
SOPD / Hospital No. : ....
Name : ....
I.D. No : ....Sex ....Age............
Dept : ....Team :.........Ward/Bed :..../......

Section I : Personal details of the maker of this advance directive

Name : .... *(please use capital letters)*

Identity Document No.: ....

Sex :   Male / Female

Date of Birth : ____/____/____
                (Day) (Month) (Year)

Home Address : ....
....

Home Tel. No. : ....
Office Tel. No. : ....
Mobile Tel. No. : ....

Section II : Background

1. I understand that the object of this directive is to minimise distress or indignity which I may suffer or create when I am terminally ill or in a persistent vegetative state or a state of irreversible coma, or in other specified end-stage irreversible life limiting condition, and to spare my medical advisers or relatives, or both, the burden of making difficult decisions on my behalf.

2. I understand that euthanasia will not be performed, nor will any unlawful instructions as to my medical treatment be followed in any circumstances, even if expressly requested.

3. I, _____ (please print name) being over the age of 18 years, revoke all previous advance directives made by me relating to my medical care and treatment (if any), and make the following advance directive of my own free will.

4. If I become terminally ill or if I am in a state of irreversible coma or in a persistent vegetative state or in other specified end-stage irreversible life limiting condition as diagnosed by my attending doctor and at least one other doctor, so that I am unable to take part in decisions about my medical care and treatment, my directives in relation to my medical care and treatment are as follows:

(Note: Complete the following by ticking the appropriate box(es) and writing your initials against that/those box(es), and drawing a line across any part you do not want to apply to you.)

---

[1] The Form was proposed by the Law Reform Commission on 16 August 2006; amended as in Food and Health Bureau Consultation Paper on 23 December 2009; modifications made and footnotes added by the Hospital Authority in May 2010 and in Jun 2014.

Rev: 10 June 2014

ADVANCE DIRECTIVE   HA 9610/MR

(A) Case 1 – Terminally ill

(Note: In this instruction –

"Terminally ill" means suffering from advanced, progressive, and irreversible disease, and failing to respond to curative therapy, having a short life expectancy in terms of days, weeks or a few months; and the application of life-sustaining treatment would only serve to postpone the moment of death, and

"Life-sustaining treatment" means any of the treatments which have the potential to postpone the patient's death and includes, for example, cardiopulmonary resuscitation, artificial ventilation, blood products, pacemakers, vasopressors, specialised treatments for particular conditions such as chemotherapy or dialysis, antibiotics when given for a potentially life-threatening infection, and artificial nutrition and hydration. (Artificial nutrition and hydration means the feeding of food and water to a person through a tube.))

- ☐ I shall not be given the following life-sustaining treatment(s):
    - ☐ Cardiopulmonary resuscitation (CPR)
    - ☐ Others: _____

    _____

- ☐ Save for basic and palliative care, I shall not be given any life-sustaining treatment[2]. Non-artificial nutrition and hydration shall, for the purposes of this form, form part of basic care.
    - ☐ However, I want to continue to receive artificial nutrition and hydration, if clinically indicated, until death is imminent and inevitable.

(B) Case 2 – Persistent vegetative state or a state of irreversible coma

(Note: In this instruction -

"Life-sustaining treatment" means any of the treatments which have the potential to postpone the patient's death and includes, for example, cardiopulmonary resuscitation, artificial ventilation, blood products, pacemakers, vasopressors, specialised treatments for particular conditions such as chemotherapy or dialysis, antibiotics when given for a potentially life-threatening infection, and artificial nutrition and hydration[3]. (Artificial nutrition and hydration means the feeding of food and water to a person through a tube.))

- ☐ I shall not be given the following life-sustaining treatment(s):
    - ☐ Cardiopulmonary resuscitation (CPR)
    - ☐ Others: _____

    _____

- ☐ Save for basic and palliative care, I shall not be given any life-sustaining treatment[4]. Non-artificial nutrition and hydration shall, for the purposes of this form, form part of basic care.
    - ☐ However, I want to continue to receive artificial nutrition and hydration, if clinically indicated, until death is imminent and inevitable.

---

[2] Care should be taken to ensure that the patient has really decided not to consent to receive "all" life-sustaining treatment.

[3] Note that to withdraw artificial nutrition and hydration (ANH) in a non-terminally ill patient who is in a persistent vegetative state or a state of irreversible coma (PVS/IC) can be contentious even in the presence of an AD. For patients presenting with such a directive and in PVS/IC, advice should be sought from the HCE/CCE and HAHO to consider whether an application to the Court is required. A patient wishing to make a directive to withdraw ANH, or to withdraw all life-sustaining treatments under this Section, should be alerted about this special caution.

[4] Care should be taken to ensure that the patient has really decided not to consent to receive "all" life-sustaining treatment.

Rev: 10 June 2014

(C) **Case 3 – Other end-stage irreversible life limiting condition, namely:** _____

(Note: In this instruction -

"Other end-stage irreversible life limiting condition" means suffering from an advanced, progressive, and irreversible condition not belonging to Case 1 or Case 2, but has reached the end-stage of the condition, limiting survival of the patient. Examples include:

    (1) patients with end-stage renal failure, end-stage motor neuron disease, or end-stage chronic obstructive pulmonary disease who may not fall into the definition of terminal illness in Case 1, because their survival may be prolonged by dialysis or assisted ventilation, and

    (2) patients with irreversible loss of major cerebral function and extremely poor functional status who do not fall into Case 2.

"Life-sustaining treatment" means any of the treatments which have the potential to postpone the patient's death and includes, for example, cardiopulmonary resuscitation, artificial ventilation, blood products, pacemakers, vasopressors, specialised treatments for particular conditions such as chemotherapy or dialysis, antibiotics when given for a potentially life-threatening infection, and artificial nutrition and hydration. (Artificial nutrition and hydration means the feeding of food and water to a person through a tube.))

☐   I shall not be given the following life-sustaining treatment(s):

    ☐   **Cardiopulmonary resuscitation (CPR)**

    ☐   **Others:** _____

    _____

☐   **Save for basic and palliative care, I shall not be given any life-sustaining treatment**[5]**. Non-artificial nutrition and hydration shall, for the purposes of this form, form part of basic care.**

    ☐   **However, I want to continue to receive artificial nutrition and hydration, if clinically indicated, until death is imminent and inevitable.**

5. I make this directive in the presence of the two witnesses named in Section III of this advance directive, who are not beneficiaries under:
    (i) my will; or
    (ii) any policy of insurance held by me; or
    (iii) any other instrument made by me or on my behalf.

6. I understand I can revoke this advance directive at anytime[6].

_____   _____
Signature of the maker of this advance directive   Date

Section III : Witnesses

Notes for witness :

    A witness must be a person who is not a beneficiary under –
    (i) the will of the maker of this advance directive; or
    (ii) any policy of insurance held by the maker of this advance directive; or
    (iii) any other instrument made by or on behalf of the maker of this advance directive.

---

[5] Care should be taken to ensure that the patient has really decided not to consent to receive "all" life-sustaining treatment.
[6] A written revocation can be directly signed on the advance directive form, or written and signed on a separate piece of paper and attached to the advance directive form.

Other Planning Tools 123

Statement of Witnesses

First Witness

(Note: This witness must be a registered medical practitioner, who, at the option of the maker of this directive, could be a doctor other than one who is treating or has treated the maker of this directive.)

(1) I, _____ (please print name) sign below as witness.

    (a) as far as I know, the maker of this directive has made the directive voluntarily; and

    (b) I have explained to the maker of this directive the nature and implications of making this directive.

(2) I declare that this directive is made and signed in my presence together with the second witness named below.

_____   _____
Signature of 1st witness   Date

Name: ....

Identity Document No. / Medical Council Registration No. [7]**:** ....

Office Address: ....

....

Office Tel. No. : ....

Second Witness

(Note: This witness must be at least 18 years of age)

(1) I, _____ (please print name) sign below as witness.

(2) I declare that this directive is made and signed in my presence together with the first witness named above, and that the first witness has, in my presence, explained to the maker of this directive the nature and implications of making this directive.

_____   _____
Signature of 2nd witness   Date

Name: ....

Identity Document No. [8]**:** ....

Home Address / Contact Address : ....

....

Home Tel. No. / Contact No. : ....

---

[7] It is not necessary for HA staff to provide the Identity Document No. / Medical Council Registration No. since staff code or address of hospital ward/unit would be sufficient for the identification of the 1st witness.

[8] It is not necessary for HA staff to provide the Identity document No. since staff code or address of hospital ward/unit would be sufficient for the identification of the 2nd witness.

Rev: 10 June 2014

8
Will or No Will?

In Chapter 7, we discussed planning tools such as EPA, ADs and the emerging CPA, which a person may consider making during his or her lifetime when he or she retains the relevant mental capacity.

The focus in this chapter will be on the making of wills. Many people, particularly those with special needs children, are concerned with whether or not they should make a will and appoint a testamentary guardian to ensure that their loved ones are cared for when they pass away. Others may consider making a will as part of their wealth and succession planning.

Before one considers whether it is necessary to execute a will, one should have a basic understanding of what would happen to his or her estate if one had not made a will.

A deceased person who died without making a will is referred to as "**Intestate**". The relevant legislation in Hong Kong relating to the distribution of the estate of the Intestate is the Intestates' Estates Ordinance (Cap 73) (**IEO**).

The IEO also covers the scenario when a person made a will but did not dispose of all of his or her property and assets in that will. In such cases, the IEO will be effective with respect to the remaining part of the person's property not disposed of in his or her will.[1]

Depending on whether the Intestate had any surviving spouse, children, parents or siblings, the estate will be distributed differently according to the provisions in the IEO.

The following common scenarios illustrate how intestacy law generally operates. These illustrations, together with the flowchart at the end of this chapter, are designed to provide readers with basic guidance when considering whether they should make a will.

---

1. Subject to the provisions under s 8 of the IEO "Application to Cases of Partial Intestacy".

1. The first question one should ask when dealing with the administration of a deceased's estate is:
   Does the deceased have a surviving spouse? If the answer is no, refer to paragraph 5 below. If the answer is yes, then one must also ask: *Does the deceased have any surviving children?* If the answer is yes, the law states that the deceased's spouse will receive HK$500,000 and half of the net estate. The surviving children, if more than one, will split the other half equally.[2]
2. If the deceased is survived by a spouse but does not have any children surviving, the next question is: *Does the deceased have any surviving parents?* If the answer is no, refer to paragraph 3 below. If the answer is yes, the spouse will receive HK$1,000,000 and half of the estate. The surviving parents of the deceased will receive the other half equally.[3]
3. If the deceased is survived by a spouse but does not have any surviving children nor any surviving parents, the next question is: *Does the deceased have any surviving siblings, nieces or nephews?* If the answer is no, refer to paragraph 4 below. If the answer is yes, the spouse will receive HK$1,000,000 and half of the estate. The siblings of the deceased will split the other half equally.
4. If the deceased is survived by a spouse but does not have any surviving children, nor any surviving parents, nor any surviving siblings, nieces or nephews, then the spouse of the deceased will receive the net estate absolutely, ie in full.
5. If the deceased does not have a surviving spouse, the next question is: *Does the deceased have any surviving children?* If the answer is no, refer to paragraph 6 below. If the answer is yes, the child will inherit the deceased's estate absolutely; if there is more than one child, the children will split the estate equally.
6. If the deceased does not have any surviving spouse nor any surviving children, the next question is: *Does the deceased have any surviving parents?* If the answer is no, refer to paragraph 7 below. If the answer is yes, the parents of the deceased will split the estate equally.
7. If the deceased does not have any surviving spouse, nor any surviving children, nor any surviving parents, the next question is: *Does the deceased have any surviving siblings, nieces or nephews?* If the answer is no, refer to paragraph 8 below. If the answer is yes, the extended relatives of the deceased will receive the deceased's estate in accordance with the IEO.[4]

---

2. Section 4(3) of the IEO.
3. Section 4(4) of the IEO.
4. Section 4(8) of the IEO.

8. If the deceased does not have any surviving spouse, nor any surviving children, nor any surviving parents, nor any surviving siblings, nieces or nephews, the deceased's estate may belong to the government as *bona vacantia*.[5]

The contents above and the flow chart at the end of the chapter are intended to provide basic guidance in relation to the intestacy law in Hong Kong and are by no means exhaustive. Please consult your solicitors and obtain proper legal advice if you are considering making a will or preparing for wealth and succession planning.

What Is a Will?

A will is a written declaration of a person's wishes in relation to his or her property intended to take effect upon his or her death.[6] The person making the will is referred to as the "**Testator**".

Section 2 of the Wills Ordinance (Cap 30) (**WO**) defines "will" to "include a codicil and any other testamentary instrument or act".

In order for a will to be valid, it must be made in accordance with section 5 of the WO; ie, it must be in writing and signed by the Testator in the presence of at least two witnesses at the same time. The witnesses must also attest and sign the will. In other words, the will must:

1) be written;[7]
2) be signed by the Testator[8] who intended to give effect to the will by his signature;[9] and
3) be signed and acknowledged by the Testator in the presence of two or more witnesses at the same time who must also have attested and signed the will.[10]

Practical Considerations

Here are some practical considerations in making a will:

---

5. Subject to the Inheritance (Provision for Family and Dependents) Ordinance (Cap 481) and s 4(9) of the IEO.
6. Rebecca Ong, *A Guide to Wills and Probate in Hong Kong* (Hong Kong: Sweet & Maxwell, 2014), para 1.002.
7. Section 5(1)(a) of the WO.
8. Ibid.
9. Section 5(1)(b) of the WO.
10. Section 5 of the WO.

1. Domicile

Your domicile as at the date of death can have implications on your tax position. Unless you elect to adopt a domicile of choice, your domicile will be the domicile you acquired at birth, generally the nationality or domicile of your father, rather than the location of your birth.

2. Appointment of executor

An executor is a person who will be in charge of administrating the Testator's estate (**Executor**). Executors are governed under the Trustee Ordinance (Cap 29) (**TO**).

Executors must be at least 21 years old at the time of administering the estate.[11] If there are children beneficiaries, you will usually need to name two persons to act as Executors.

A Testator can name up to a maximum of four[12] persons to act as Executors. Once appointed, the Executors must, if so appointed, jointly administer the estate.

3. Contents of a will

The contents of a will can include arrangements as to the funeral, personal items, legacies and distribution of the residue of the estate.

Personal items can be left to certain persons, ie beneficiaries. If the Testator wishes to leave specific items or gifts to a particular beneficiary, he or she should make specific provisions in the will; if not, the gift will fall into the residual estate and be distributed among the beneficiaries under the direction of the Executor or sold with the proceeds falling into the cash residue.

Legacies are specific arrangements of money, shares or property. These include any monetary gifts made to charities.

The residual estate is the remaining portion of the estate after payment of funeral expenses, estate administration expenses, duties, debts and any specific gifts or legacies. The residue usually consists of the bulk of the estate. The Testator can make arrangements as to the distribution of the residual estate in the will.

---

11. Section 36 and 37 of the TO.
12. Section 36 of the TO.

4. Guardianship of minor children

If you have minor children, you may also wish to appoint a person to be your testamentary guardian to have custody of your children in case of the death of your spouse. The testamentary guardian may be the same person as your Executor, or you may name a different person so that there is no potential conflict of interest relating to the discretionary payments from the trustee to the guardian. However, in circumstances where there is dispute over the custody of the children, the court will make the decision as to who will be awarded custody based on the children's best interests. Thus, if the parents are divorced, the appointment of the testamentary guardian cannot displace the rights of the surviving legal parent.

5. Children under disability

If one of the beneficiaries is mentally incapacitated or a child with a disability, you may wish to discuss with your solicitors to make a special trust provision for these beneficiaries.

6. Obligations to maintain others

A will shall be revoked by your marriage unless special provisions are built into your will. If you have any obligations to maintain anyone including but not limited to a cohabitee or former spouse or common law spouse, whether as a result of a separation agreement or court order, these obligations may survive your death.

It is therefore important to seek appropriate legal advice in planning your will and overall family wealth succession planning.

Solicitors' Role in the Preparation and Execution of Wills

In a recent judgment, Mr Justice Cheung JA set out his views on the role of a solicitor in the preparation and execution of a will, which he observed were particularly important in a society like Hong Kong where the population is ageing and more people have shed their traditional mindset of not having a will prepared during their lifetime on superstitious grounds.[13]

He listed the following matters (which are not exhaustive) into which a solicitor should enquire well before the day appointed for the execution of the will:

---

13. See the Court of Appeal judgment dated 20 April, CACC No 177/2017, [2018] HKCA 210.

1. the age of the Testator;
2. the Testator's health condition;
3. whether the Testator has a surviving spouse;
4. the number of children and grandchildren the Testator has;
5. whether there is someone other than the Testator's immediate family members dependent on the Testator for support;
6. the beneficiaries that the Testator would like to provide for;
7. the Testator's properties;
8. whether the Testator has made a previous will;
9. whether the Testator understands that the new will would revoke the previous will; and
10. whether the Testator understands the difference between the new and the previous will.

It is also good practice for a solicitor, when drawing up a will for an aged or seriously ill Testator, to have the will witnessed or approved by a medical practitioner who should record his examination of the Testator, and to ensure that the Testator is capable of "understanding the nature of the act and its effects"; "understanding the extent of the property being disposed of"; and "able to comprehend and appreciate the claims to which a person making a will ought to give effect".[14]

Statutory Will

Is it possible for a person who is mentally incapacitated to make a will?

The court has the power under the MHO[15] to give directions as to the execution of a will for the MIP, making any provision for that person as if he or she were not mentally incapacitated. This is referred to as a statutory will.

Mr Justice Lam (as he then was) set out the requirements and considerations the court would take into account in considering whether to give directions to execute a statutory will for MIPs under the MHO[16] in the case of *Re CYL* [2007] 4 HKLRD 218.

Lam J explained that the court's power to make an order or give directions for the execution of a statutory will for the MIP could not be exercised unless it had reasonable grounds to believe that the patient lacked testamentary capacity.[17] The court does not have to make a finding as to the person's

---

14. See the judgment of Chow J in [2017] 4 HKLRD 284, 4 July 2017.
15. Section 10B(1)(e) of the MHO.
16. Section 10B(4)(b) of the MHO.
17. See para 16 of *Re CYL*.

testamentary capacity; it only has to have reasonable belief that the person lacks testamentary capacity.[18]

Once the court is satisfied that the threshold[19] is met, it will consider whether it should exercise its discretion to authorize the execution of a will on behalf of the MIP.[20]

In considering whether it should exercise its discretion, the court will take into account various factors under the MHO,[21] under which the paramount consideration is the requirements of the MIP, ie what is in the MIP's best interests.[22]

Thus, if the court decides to exercise its discretion to execute a will on behalf of the MIP, the court must seek to make the will with provisions which the MIP himself or herself[23] would have made if he or she was restored to full mental capacity, memory and foresight and with sound legal advice available.[24]

---

18. See para 23 of *Re CYL*.
19. Section 10B(4)(b) of the MHO.
20. See para 25 of *Re CYL*.
21. Section 10A(2) of the MHO.
22. See paras 31–32 of *Re CYL*.
23. As opposed to a hypothetical person: see para 35 of *Re CYL*.
24. See paras 34 to 38 of *Re CYL*, in particular para 36.

Figure 8.1: If the Deceased Did Not Make a Will

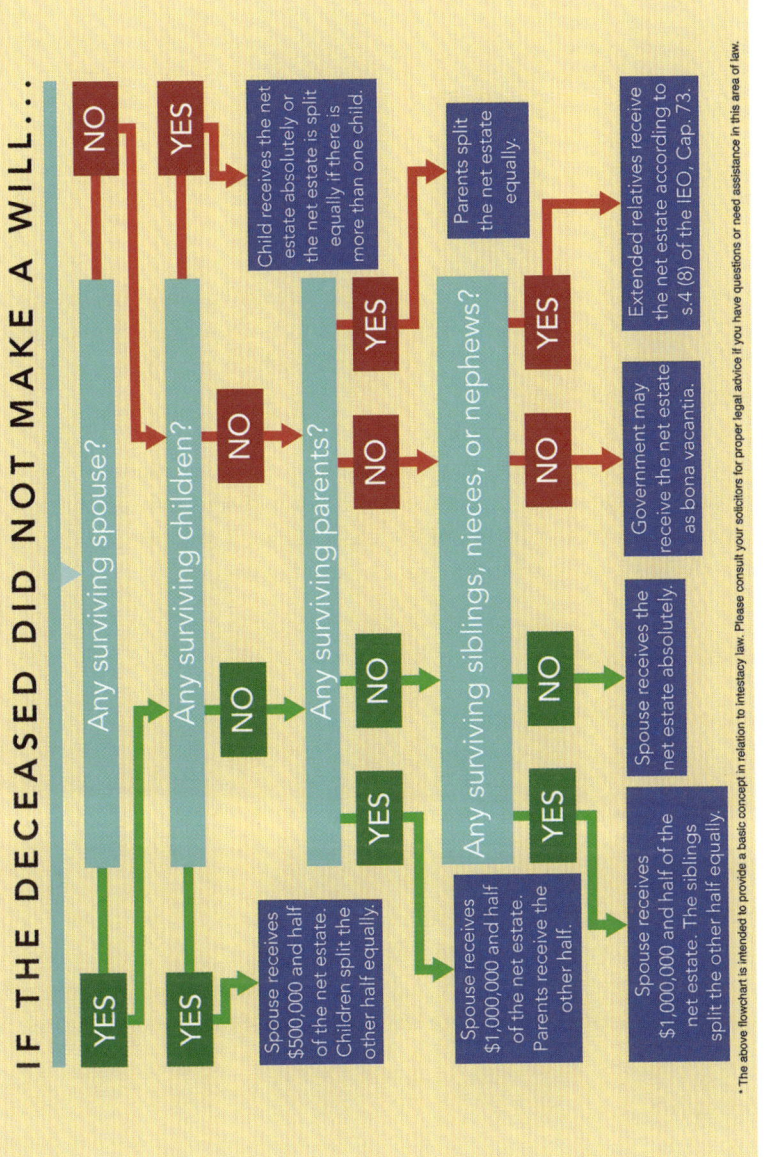

9
Hong Kong and Beyond

In this chapter, I will briefly describe the relevant mental health law regimes in the United Kingdom and Singapore and note some of the areas in Hong Kong's current mental health law regime which may need to be reviewed sooner rather than later.

Since this is a guidebook for carers of MIPs and not intended to be an in-depth academic work, the discussions here are intended only to raise community awareness and stimulate further discussion among professionals involved in caring for mentally incapacitated and special needs persons under Hong Kong's current mental health law regime.

United Kingdom

The Court of Protection

In the United Kingdom, there is a unique, specialist court known as the Court of Protection with jurisdiction to handle matters relating to MIPs under the Mental Capacity Act 2005 (**MCA**).

The Court of Protection has power to make declarations as to the mental capacity of a person, to appoint and remove deputies who are in charge of the MIP's personal welfare and affairs, to adjudicate on disputes relating to powers of attorney, and to make other judicial decisions regarding the property and financial affairs or health and welfare of incapacitated adults.

The Deputy

The functions of a deputy in the UK are similar to that of the Committee and guardian **combined** in Hong Kong.

If an MIP has not appointed an attorney under a lasting power of attorney (**LPA**), an application can be made to the Court of Protection to appoint a deputy.[1] Deputies act as agents[2] of the MIP in relation to the MIP's health, welfare and financial affairs. Deputies must be at least 18 years old[3] and are usually relatives or close friends of the MIP.[4] A trust corporation can only be a deputy for an MIP in relation to his or her financial affairs, not in relation to health and welfare of the MIP.[5]

Section 20 of the MCA sets out the restrictions on the powers of deputies. For example, the deputy must act in the best interests of the MIP.[6]

The Court of Protection may also require the deputy to provide security over the assets which the deputy is managing[7] so as to offer additional protection to the MIP. The Court has discretion as to the amount of such security.[8]

The deputy is also subject to supervision of the Office of the Public Guardian (**OPG**)[9] and is required to produce reports to the OPG.[10]

The Office of the Public Guardian

The Public Guardian is appointed by the Lord Chancellor.[11] The Public Guardian has an administrative role.[12] There is no equivalent of the OPG in Hong Kong. Its functions include supervising the deputies, maintaining a register of LPAs and orders appointing deputies, and directing visitors to visit attorneys and deputies.

There are "**General Visitors**" and "**Special Visitors**".[13] General Visitors do not have medical qualifications and undertake routine inspection on deputies to ascertain if the deputies understand and are carrying out their duties properly. Special Visitors are usually medical practitioners. They have to be appointed by the Lord Chancellor. Special Visitors are only required to visit deputies when there is an issue of capacity of an MIP.

---

1. Section 19 of the MCA.
2. Section 19(6) of the MCA.
3. Section 19(1) of the MCA.
4. A. Kimberley Dayton (ed), *Comparative Perspectives on Adult Guardianship* (Durham, North Carolina: Carolina Academic Press, 2014), p 144.
5. Section 19(1)(b) of the MCA and ibid.
6. Section 20(6) of the MCA.
7. Section 19(9)(a) of the MCA.
8. A. Kimberley Dayton (ed), *Comparative Perspectives on Adult Guardianship* (Durham, North Carolina: Carolina Academic Press, 2014), p 145.
9. Section 58(1)(c) of the MCA.
10. Sections 19(9)(b) and 58(1)(f) of the MCA.
11. Section 57(2) of the MCA.
12. A. Kimberley Dayton (ed), *Comparative Perspectives on Adult Guardianship* (Durham, North Carolina: Carolina Academic Press, 2014), p 146.
13. Ibid., p 147 and see s 61 of the MCA.

The OPG will also publish guidelines to facilitate the functions of the OPG, including guidelines for deputies,[14] and investigate complaints of deputies and attorneys.[15]

The Attorney

In the UK, since 1 October 2007, enduring powers of attorney (**EPA**) are replaced by the LPA. Attorneys can obtain assistance from the Court of Protection but would not be supervised by the Court or the OPG.[16]

The powers of the attorney appointed under an LPA may be restricted. For example, an attorney under the LPA can only make gifts on customary occasions to persons who are related or connected to the MIP or to any charity which the MIP may have been expected to make gifts to. The value of the gift must also be reasonable in the context of the MIP's estate.[17]

The major differences between an EPA and LPA are that an LPA can be registered by the donor or the attorney before the donor becomes mentally incapacitated and that an LPA can be revoked by a donor if he or she has capacity to do so without the requirement of a confirmation from the Court of Protection.[18]

Singapore

In Singapore, the Mental Capacity Act 2008 (**MCA of Singapore**) came into force in March 2010. The MCA of Singapore is similar to the UK's MCA.[19]

The Court

Similar to Hong Kong, it seems that there is no designated Court of Protection to handle matters for persons who lack capacity in Singapore.

---

14. Section 58(1)(i) of the MCA.
15. Section 58(1)(h) of the MCA.
16. See The Law Commission (LAW COM.No.122), Report on *The Incapacitated Principal* (London, July 1983), para 4.78, p 44, and A. Kimberley Dayton (ed), *Comparative Perspectives on Adult Guardianship* (Durham, North Carolina: Carolina Academic Press, 2014), p 150.
17. Section 12(2) of the MCA.
18. Sections 9(2) and 13(2) of the MCA and see A. Kimberley Dayton (ed), *Comparative Perspectives on Adult Guardianship* (Durham, North Carolina: Carolina Academic Press, 2014), p 150.
19. Roger C. Ho, Cyrus S. Ho, Nusrat Khan, and Ee Heok Kua, "An Overview of Mental Health Law in Singapore" (2015), *BJPsych International*. https://www.ncbi.nlm.nih.gov/pmc/articles/PMC5618915/

The High Court or a Family Court[20] of Singapore has the power to make declarations as to whether a person lacks capacity,[21] to make orders on behalf of an MIP in relation to his personal welfare and/or property and affairs,[22] to appoint deputies to make decisions relating to the MIP's personal welfare and/or property affairs,[23] and to make decisions relating to powers of attorneys.[24]

The Deputy

The role of a deputy in Singapore is similar to that of the Committee and guardian in Hong Kong and the deputy in the UK.

Similar to the UK, an application can be made to the High Court or a Family Court for an appointment of a deputy.[25] A deputy acts as an agent of the MIP to make decisions for the MIP on personal welfare and property matters.[26] Unlike the UK, deputies in Singapore must be at least 21 years old.[27]

The powers of a deputy are restricted under section 25 of the MCA of Singapore. The restrictions are similar to that of the UK's MCA. Likewise, the High Court or a Family Court may require a deputy to report to Singapore's Public Guardian and to give security over the assets that the deputy is managing.[28]

The Office of the Public Guardian

In Singapore, the OPG is appointed by the Minister. Its functions[29] are largely similar to those of the UK.

However, the OPG of Singapore has the additional powers to investigate any contravention of any provisions of the MCA of Singapore[30] and to require any person who has information of an MIP to furnish such information to it.[31]

---

20. Section 2 of the MCA of Singapore.
21. Section 19 of the MCA of Singapore.
22. Sections 20, 22, and 23 of the MCA of Singapore.
23. Sections 20, 24, and 25 of the MCA of Singapore.
24. Sections 17 and 18 of the MCA of Singapore.
25. Section 24 of the MCA of Singapore.
26. Section 24(7) of the MCA of Singapore.
27. Section 24(1) of the MCA of Singapore.
28. Section 24(10) of the MCA of Singapore.
29. Section 31(1) of the MCA of Singapore.
30. Section 31(1)(i) and (j) of the MCA of Singapore.
31. Section 32 of the MCA of Singapore.

The Attorney

In Singapore, a donor can make an LPA in relation to his personal welfare and property and affairs.[32] Unlike the UK, the attorney must be 21 years old.[33]

The powers of an attorney in Singapore are different from those in the UK. Gifts can be made if the LPA contains an express authorization stating the same, and if the value of the gift is not specified in the LPA, the attorney may make gifts of a reasonable value taking into account all circumstances and in the best interests of the MIP.[34]

The donor can revoke the LPA when he still possesses capacity without an application to the court.[35]

Hong Kong

In Hong Kong, *there is no Court of Protection* specifically set up to handle matters relating to MIPs. Instead, the MHO provides that the Court of First Instance has power to make declarations as to the mental capacity of a person under Part II of the MHO and to make orders in relation to the management of financial affairs of the MIP.

The Registrar of the Court of First Instance will receive annual accounts submitted by a Committee and approve the accounts after making necessary requisitions and finding them to be a true, accurate and complete picture of the financial position of the estate of the MIP.

Apart from approving the annual accounts, the Court may require the Committee to provide security and make an order for the remuneration of the Committee out of the MIP's estate as the Court deems fit.

Thus, while professional Committees such as solicitors and accountants may be regulated by their respective professional bodies, the Committees appointed are not otherwise supervised by the Court of First Instance or any other office and may not be aware of their statutory duties.

In addition, Hong Kong *does not have an Office of Public Guardian and/or Public Trustee.*

The power to review a Guardianship Order rests with the Guardianship Board which deals with the welfare of the MIP and limits the financial power of a guardian, whereas the management of property and financial affairs rests with the Court of First Instance.

With the ageing population and increase in the number of mentally incapacitated persons, support for the Guardianship Board and Court of

---

32. Section 11 of the MCA of Singapore.
33. Section 12(1) of the MCA of Singapore.
34. Section 14 of the MCA of Singapore. See ss 13 and 14 for other restrictions of powers.
35. Section 15(1) of the MCA of Singapore.

First Instance needs to be enhanced. Currently, the support work for the Guardianship Board and Court of First Instance is shared between the Director of Social Welfare and the Official Solicitor. This should be expanded to cater for the increasing workload.

In Hong Kong, there is *no regime of LPAs*. An EPA can only be made in relation to the financial affairs of the donor[36] and it can only be revoked if the donor has capacity or with confirmation of the court.[37]

With the emerging continuing power of attorney, there is a proposal to extend the attorney's power to cover directions in relation to the donor's personal care as well as financial matters. The Law Reform Commission of Hong Kong (**LRC**) in fact examined the deficiencies in this area of law and proposed a review of the same back in 2006, but the consultation paper on the Continuing Powers of Attorney Bill was only issued in December 2017, almost 12 years after the LRC's report was published.

---

36. Section 8 of the EPAO.
37. Section 13(1)(c) of the EPAO.

10
The Way Forward

So, what is the way forward for Hong Kong?

Here are a few points to consider.

First, there is no consolidated statutory body to govern and supervise the various roles and work of the guardian, Committee and attorneys, be it the enduring power of attorney or the proposed continuing power of attorney.

There is also no Court of Protection to protect mentally incapacitated persons under guardianship or generally, and no Office of the Public Guardian or Public Trustee (Advocate) Office. The work is currently shared between the Court of First Instance and Guardianship Board with support from the Director of Social Welfare and the Official Solicitor.

Further, although there are many excellent initiatives undertaken by government and non-government bodies, these initiatives may not be easily accessible to the public and would undoubtedly benefit from some further consolidated effort to promote and strengthen the existing services and resources in order to meet the demands of a rapidly ageing population.

Hence, there is an urgent need for fundamental reform of the mental health law and guardianship regime to enable Hong Kong to meet the challenges of the coming decades.

Suggestions on Reform

1. Consolidation of existing initiatives

It is encouraging that the Hong Kong government has, in response to the ageing population and demands from the public for enhanced support to elderly persons suffering from dementia and their carers, made significant progress to promote and strengthen mental health and welfare services for special needs persons.

In January 2016, the Department of Health launched a three-year territory-wide "Joyful@HK" campaign to promote mental health. The objectives of the campaign were to increase public engagement in promoting mental well-being and enhance public knowledge and understanding of mental health.

In February 2017, a two-year pilot scheme steered by the Food and Health Bureau in collaboration with the Hospital Authority and Social Welfare Department on dementia community support services for the elderly, entitled the "Dementia Community Support Scheme (Pilot Scheme)", was launched.

Further, according to a Legislative Council paper published on 28 March 2017, the government has adopted a multi-disciplinary and cross-sectoral approach in the provision of holistic care to persons with dementia.

In respect of educating the public, the Hospital Authority has also made the information relating to dementia, medical care and community resources available on its one-stop information platform, the smart patient website.[1]

The Community Legal Information Centre (**CLIC**), organized by the Law and Technology Centre jointly run by the Faculty of Law and Department of Computer Science of the University of Hong Kong, has set up various bilingual websites to provide quick internet guide for the general public to find out relevant legal information, including support for special needs persons and their carers. There is also a senior CLIC website specifically targeting the elderly in Hong Kong to assist them in seeking free or subsidized legal assistance.

However, there is a continuous need to push for consolidated efforts by different departments, including the Food and Health Bureau, Home Affairs Bureau, Labour and Welfare Bureau, Department of Health, Hospital Authority, Official Solicitor's Office, Social Welfare Department, Commissioner for Elderly, Commissioner for Rehabilitation and the emerging Commissioner for Children, to promote and strengthen the existing mental health and welfare services in the climate of a rapidly increasing ageing population.

The Hong Kong community would certainly benefit from a consolidated effort by the various government bureaux and departments together with non-government organizations, because currently the existing facilities and services for the elderly and special needs persons are rather fragmented and difficult for carers and family members to locate.

---

1. A list of government and non-government resources is included in Appendix II to this guidebook.

2. Establishment of a Court of Protection and Office of the Public Guardian and/or Public Trustee (Advocate)

Establishing a Court of Protection to adjudicate disputes relating to attorneys and other judicial decisions regarding the property and financial affairs or health and welfare of incapacitated adults would better equip the judiciary to handle the significant increase in the number of cases foreseeable in the coming years.

At the same time, consideration should be given to set up an independent Office of the Public Guardian and/or Public Trustee (Advocate) to expand the powers of the Guardianship Board.

3. Amendment of unclear terms in current mental health laws

There is a need to amend the definitions of certain terminology in the current legislation so that it is more in line with international standards to provide better care for special needs persons while respecting their liberty and dignity.

For example, "mental incapacity" is defined as a "mental disorder" or "mental handicap" under section 2 of the MHO. "Mental disorder" is further defined as:

> (a) mental illness; (b) a state of arrested or incomplete development of mind which amounts to a significant impairment of intelligence and social functioning which is associated with abnormally aggressive or seriously irresponsible conduct on the part of the person concerned; (c) psychopathic disorder; or (d) any other disorder or disability of mind which does not amount to mental handicap.

However, the MHO does not provide further explanation as to what would be considered "mental illness" or "any other disorder or disability of mind which does not amount to mental handicap".[2]

A significant burden is therefore placed on the medical practitioner to diagnose whether the person in question has a mental illness and/or other form of disability of the mind.[3] In fact, there has not been a clear definition of "mental disorder" since the MHO was first enacted in 1960.[4] It is therefore suggested that "mental disorder" be defined in a more detailed manner to reflect contemporary understandings of mental health.

---

2. The Law Reform Commission of Hong Kong, Report on Substitute Decision-making and Advance Directives in Relation to Medical Treatment (Hong Kong: Printing Department, August 2006), para 6.3, p 69.
3. Ibid., para 6.4, p 70.
4. Ibid., paras 6.11 and 6.13, p 73.

Conclusion

The number of single elderly in Hong Kong is forecast to rise to 1.13 million by 2064.[5] Around 1 in 10 people aged 65 years old or above and around 1 in 3 people aged 80 or above will likely have dementia, a common cause of mental incapacity. Hong Kong must be prepared for the impact this will have on the community.

Let's work together to improve education and promote awareness of mental health, elderly and special needs issues; to provide training to detect and prevent mental deterioration and physical, emotional and financial abuse against mentally incapacitated persons; to plan for rehabilitation; and to utilise advance care planning tools for a better community.

I hope that after reading this guidebook you are more aware of the mental health regime and resources in Hong Kong. The legislators are urged to continue to push for a more advanced legal framework and social support system to protect the physical and financial well-being of special needs children, adults and elderly persons.

THE TIME TO ACT IS NOW.

---

5. "The 'dementia tsunami' and why Hong Kong isn't ready to cope with expected surge in cases as population ages", *South China Morning Post*, 16 April 2018.

Appendix I
Useful Glossary of Legal and Medical Terms

Legal Definitions under Hong Kong Ordinances

1. **Certified Patient** (實證病人) means a person who is detained in a mental hospital in accordance with the provisions of section 36 of the Mental Health Ordinance (Cap 136) (**MHO**).[1]
2. **Committee of the Estate** (產業受託監管人) means a committee appointed by the Court pursuant to section 11 of the MHO to do all such things in relation to the property and affairs of the mentally incapacitated person as the court orders or directs it to do.
3. **Enduring Power of Attorney** (持久授權書) means a power conferred on the attorney to act in relation to the property and financial affairs of the donor, where such power is not revoked by reason of any subsequent mental incapacity of the donor.[2]
4. **Guardian** (監護人) means a person appointed by the Guardianship Board under a Guardianship Order to be a guardian of a mentally incapacitated person who has attained the age of 18 years.[3]
5. **General Power of Attorney** (一般授權書), as set out in the schedule under the Powers of Attorney Ordinance, operates to confer:
   (a) on the donee of the power; or
   (b) if there is more than one donee, on the donees acting jointly or acting jointly and severally, authority to do on behalf of the donor anything which he can lawfully do by an attorney.[4]
6. **Mental Disorder** (精神紊亂) means:
   (a) mental illness;

---

1. See s 2 of the MHO.
2. See ss 2, 5 and 8 of the Enduring Powers of Attorney Ordinance (Cap 501).
3. See s 2 and Part IVB of the MHO.
4. See s 7 of the Powers of Attorney Ordinance (Cap 31).

(b) a state of arrested or incomplete development of mind which amounts to a significant impairment of intelligence and social functioning which is associated with abnormally aggressive or seriously irresponsible conduct on the part of the person concerned;
(c) psychopathic disorder; or
(d) any other disorder or disability of mind which does not amount to mental handicap.[5]

7. **Mentally Disordered Person** (精神紊亂的人) means a person suffering from mental disorder.[6]
8. **Mental Handicap** (弱智) means sub-average general intellectual functioning with deficiencies in adaptive behaviour.[7]
9. **Mentally Handicapped Person** (弱智人士) means a person who is or appears to be mentally handicapped.[8]
10. **Mental Incapacity** (精神上無行為能力) means:
    (a) mental disorder; or
    (b) mental handicap.[9]
11. **Mentally Incapacitated Person** (精神上無行為能力的人) means:
    (a) for the purpose of Part II of the MHO, a person who is incapable, by reason of mental incapacity, of managing and administering his property and affairs; or
    (b) for all other purposes, a patient or mentally handicapped person, as the case may be.[10]
12. **Patient** (病人) means a person suffering or appearing to be suffering from mental disorder.[11]
13. **Patient Under Observation** (接受觀察病人) means a person who is detained in a mental hospital in accordance with the provisions of sections 31 or 32 of the MHO.[12]
14. **Psychopathic Disorder** (精神病理障礙) means a persistent disorder or disabling of personality (whether or not including significant impairment of intelligence) which results in abnormally aggressive or seriously irresponsible conduct on the part of the person concerned.[13]

---

5. See s 2 of the MHO.
6. Ibid.
7. Ibid.
8. Ibid.
9. Ibid.
10. See ss 2 and 11 of the MHO.
11. See s 2 of the MHO.
12. Ibid.
13. Ibid.

Medical Definitions (on Common Causes of Mental Incapacity)[14]

1. **Alzheimer's Disease** (阿滋海默症), the most common type of dementia, is a chronic neurodegenerative disease resulting in cognitive and functional decline.
2. **Autism** (自閉症), a neurodevelopmental disorder, is characterized by:
   (a) persistent deficits in social communication and social interaction across multiple contexts, ie verbal/non-verbal/social-emotional reciprocity; and
   (b) restricted, repetitive patterns of behaviour, interests, or activities.
   The person with autism can be with or without accompanying intellectual impairment.
3. **Bipolar Disorder** (躁鬱症) is a major mood disorder characterized by episodes of mania, depression, or mixed mood. Characteristics of the manic phase are excessive emotional displays, such as excitement, elation, euphoria, or in some cases irritability accompanied by hyperactivity, boisterousness, impaired ability to concentrate, decreased need for sleep, and seemingly unbounded energy etc.
4. **Delusions** (妄想) are fixed beliefs that are not amenable to change in light of conflicting evidence. Their content may include a variety of themes (eg persecutory, referential, somatic, religious or grandiose ones).
5. **Dementia (or major neurocognitive disorders)** (認知障礙症), is characterized by a significant cognitive decline from a previous level of performance in one or more cognitive domains/ higher cortical functions (ie complex attention, executive function, learning and memory, language, perceptual-motor, or social cognition). Also, the cognitive deficits are significant enough to interfere with independence in everyday activities.
6. **Epilepsy** (癲癇) is a chronic neurological disorder that causes unprovoked, recurrent seizures. Seizures are sudden abnormal changes in the brain's electrical activity, resulting in periods of unusual behaviour/ sensations/change in mental state/loss of consciousness.
7. **Schizophrenia** (精神分裂症) is a chronic serious mental illness in which people interpret reality abnormally. Schizophrenia may result in some combination of hallucination, delusions, disorganized thinking (also known as formal thought disorder), disordered behaviour which impairs daily functioning, and can be disabling.
8. **Stroke** (中風), also known as **cerebrovascular accident (CVA)**, is a medical emergency in which there is sudden death of brain cells due to lack of oxygen when the blood flow to the brain is impaired by either

---

14. For further reading on the following definitions, please refer to *Mosby's Medical Dictionary*, 10th Edition.

blockage (ie ischemia) or rupture (ie haemorrhage) of brain artery. Symptoms of a stroke depend on the area of the brain affected. The most common symptom is weakness or paralysis of one side of the body or impaired sensation. Speech, swallowing, balance, and vision can also be affected.

Appendix II
Useful List of Government and Non-government Resources Available in Hong Kong

Government Resources

1. Smart Patient Website (https://www21.ha.org.hk/smartpatient/SPW/en-US/Home/)
2. Smart Elders (https://www21.ha.org.hk/smartpatient/SmartElders/en-US/Welcome/)
3. Joyful@HK (https://www.joyfulathk.hk/en/index.asp)
4. Residential Care Services for the Elderly, Social Welfare Department (https://www.swd.gov.hk/en/index/site_pubsvc/page_elderly/sub_residentia/)
5. Elderly Health Service (http://www.elderly.gov.hk/eindex.html)
6. Dementia Community Support Scheme (http://www.hpdo.gov.hk/en/dcss_index.html)
7. Standardised Care Need Assessment Mechanism for Elderly Services (https://www.swd.gov.hk/en/index/site_pubsvc/page_elderly/sub_standardis/)
8. Elderly Commission (http://www.elderlycommission.gov.hk/en/About_Us/Introduction.html)

Non-government Resources

1. Senior CLIC (http://s100.hk/en/)
2. Community Legal Information Centre (http://www.clic.org.hk/en/)
3. Hong Kong Alzheimer's Disease Association (http://www.hkada.org.hk/en/)
4. Autism Partnership (http://www.autismpartnership.com.hk/en/)
5. The Hong Kong Down Syndrome Association (http://www.hk-dsa.org.hk/?lang=en)
6. Senior Citizen Home Safety Association (https://www.schsa.org.hk/en/home/index.html)

7. New Life Psychiatric Rehabilitation Association (https://www.nlpra.org.hk/default.aspx)
8. St. James' Settlement (https://sjs.org.hk/en/front/front.php)
9. Wai Ji Christian Service (http://www.wjcs.org.hk/Eng/en_m1_1.aspx)
10. Haven of Hope Christian Service (https://www.hohcs.org.hk/)
11. Hong Chi Association (http://www.hongchi.org.hk/en_about_intro.asp)
12. Heep Hong Society (https://www.heephong.org/eng)
13. The Hong Kong Society for the Aged (http://www.sage.org.hk/?lang=en-US)
14. Love Your Brain (https://www.loveyourbrain.org.hk/en)
15. Joyful Return (https://www.e1668.hk/?lang=en)
16. Charles K Kao Foundation for Alzheimer's Disease (https://www.charleskaofoundation.org/#!/)
17. The Boys' & Girls' Clubs Association of Hong Kong (https://www.bgca.org.hk/?locale=en-US)
18. Sau Po Centre on Ageing, The University of Hong Kong (http://ageing.hku.hk/)
19. The Institute of Active Ageing, The Hong Kong Polytechnic University (http://iaa.apss.polyu.edu.hk/)
20. MIP Care Resources Connect (www.mipconnecthk.org)

Day Care/Residential Homes

1. Jockey Club Centre for Positive Ageing (https://www.jccpa.org.hk/en/home/index.html)
2. Caritas Hong Kong – Elderly Centres/Day Care Centres/Residential Homes (www.caritas.org.hk/en/service/elderly/location)
3. Kin Chi Dementia Care Support Service Centre (https://cc.sjs.org.hk/?route=services-detail&sid=35&lang=3)
4. The Hong Kong Anti-Cancer Society Jockey Club Cancer Rehabilitation Centre (https://www.jccrc.org.hk/en/)
5. Jockey Club Blissful Villa (http://www.tungwahcsd.org/en/our-services/elderly-services/care-attention-home/JCBV/introduction)
6. Yan Oi Tong Clarea Au Eldergarten (Chinese only) (http://www.clareaaueldergarten.yot.org.hk/)
7. Wan Chai Methodist Centre for the Elderly (Chinese only) (https://www.methodist-centre.com/decc/tc/home)
8. Kwong Yum Care Home (Chinese only) (http://hkcccu.kych.org.hk/)